BOOK of DAYS

The poster in the image reads:

IRISH NATIONAL FORESTERS
Branch:—BROS. PEARSE, No. 1,114
GRAND CONCERT
WILL BE GIVEN IN THE
ABBEY THEATRE
Under the Auspices of the above
On Sunday, 13th May, '28
When the following Pick of Dublin's Talent will appear:
Miss L. MOONEY'S No. 1 & 2 TROUPES
In A Classical Acrobatic and Laughable Dutch Dancing Act

Humorists	Vocalists	Dancers
George BLACK	Fred DUNNE	
Max WHELAN	J. J. MANNING	
Pat WHELAN	W. MURPHY	George LEONARD
Joseph CHEEVERS		

THE BIRTHDAY PARTY

2004 marks the centenary of the Abbey Theatre and between these covers we acknowledge and celebrate the many actors, writers, directors and designers who have contributed to the countless magical nights on our stage. In telling their tales they have mapped the story of our country in the imagination of its people. That has been an intangible but priceless gift which has placed the Abbey in the forefront of Irish cultural life. This Book of Days also celebrates the glories of Irish drama in the twentieth century and the repertoire of the world famous theatre company which has become synonymous with the best of that drama.

The Abbey Theatre was born in controversy and controversy

has been its bedfellow throughout its turbulent first century. However, in spite of riots, fire, financial ups and downs, the waxing and waning of its public and critical popularity the Abbey survives as a powerful voice of the evolving nation. It has, to quote the famous words of Joyce "forged in the smithy" of its soul "the uncreated conscience" of the race.

This Book of Days salutes the triumph and imperfection of the way and the resilience of the wayfarers.

Ben Barnes
Artistic Director.

THE THEATRE IN ABBEY STREET

Visitors from abroad as well as from other parts of Ireland often declare themselves perplexed that the National Theatre should be known as 'the Abbey'. One overseas academic was heard to explain that the name came from the noble ideal of 'a building that would be seen as a place of theatrical worship, a shrine to the drama'. The reality is much more prosaic: as most Dubliners know, a former theatre on the site was known as 'the theatre in Abbey Street'. It had had many incarnations; when the National Theatre Society took over the premises in 1904 it was known as "The Mechanics' Theatre" and was principally a venue for trade union meetings and entertainment. Its 526 seat auditorium was adjacent to the rear of a fine two-storey bank which fronted on Marlborough Street. The architect Joseph Holloway converted it to form the Abbey Theatre's entrance, foyer and offices. Funds for the enterprise were provided by Annie Horniman, a wealthy English heiress, an admirer of W. B. Yeats and part of his circle in London. Horniman continued to subsidise the theatre annually until 1910.

High Ambition

The Abbey site had at one time included the city morgue. The wits of Dublin were keen to point out that this boded ill for a theatre that intended to present a life-enhancing image

Brendan Conroy and Fiona McGeown in the 2000 production of Translations *by Brian Friel.*

PHOTO: TOM LAWLOR

of Ireland. This image was principally the creation of William Butler Yeats, a poet with a highly developed sense of his country's, and his own, cultural destiny. Yeats, together with Augusta Gregory, an aristocratic widow of literary leanings and stern organisational skills and Edward Martyn, a wealthy patron of the arts, were the founders of the theatre. At that time, there was a popular professional theatre in Dublin producing patriotic drama, including work by Dion Boucicault. The "Abbey Three" chose to ignore this, referring obliquely to 'buffoonery and easy sentiment' and declaring that they would create a theatre where the plays would be written 'with a high ambition' expressing 'the deeper thoughts and emotions of Ireland'. The precepts of their Irish Literary Theatre now seem extravagantly arcane, yet this group possessed the creative instinct and intellectual drive to mastermind a movement which would result in a spectacularly adventurous theatre that in the course of time would embrace strands of national life, customs, and attitudes to an extent that would not have been foreseen.

An Abbey Style

The Irish Literary Theatre, which imported its players from England, evolved into the National Theatre Society. The

Jim Norton and Eamon Kelly in the 1988 production of Boss Grady's Boys *by Sebastian Barry.*

PHOTO: FERGUS BOURKE

directors came to comprehend that a specifically Irish style of acting was required. The work of writers who sought their themes in the smallholdings of West Cork and on the mountaintops of Cooley demanded the natural delivery of vernacular speech. The brothers Frank and Willie Fay, who had run a small semi-professional company, were entrusted with creating that style. Frank Fay had previously been vociferous in newspaper articles about the absurdity of English actors being cast in Irish parts; Willie Fay had appeared on stage in patriotic melodramas and welcomed new and superior quality material. Though the directors of the Abbey ultimately quarreled with the brothers, causing them to resign in 1909, the Fays bequeathed a performance ethos that for many years was recognised as 'the Abbey style of acting'.

Travelling Players

The young company was frequently on tour abroad during the early years of the 20th century. The first visits to Britain resulted in an extraordinarily complimentary response from the London press. Plays that portrayed peasants, fisherfolk and dwellers in impoverished urban landscapes were seen as undeniably avant garde. Their authors were praised for the use of the kind of rich and vivid language that had been absent from the British stage since Jacobean times. The Irish novelist and critic George Moore wrote admiringly of 'great literature in a barbarous idiom'.

Some of the plays chosen for a thirty city tour of the United States in 1911-12 proved too strong for the immigré Irish community, as they had proved to be at home in Dublin: there were calls for the banning of Synge's *The Playboy of the Western World* and T.C. Murray's *Birthright*. In Philadephia the actors were arrested for 'presenting plays likely to corrupt the morals of good citizens' but when the case came up in court it was dismissed. These tours were essential to the economic survival of the company in its early years and were revived in the thirties. In 1937-38 the players were on the road in North America for a punishing eight months. Critics in Ireland referred to the general exhaustion of the company, and the public, not unreasonably enquired why the best actors such as Eileen Crowe, Maureen Delany, May Craig, Barry Fitzgerald and F.J. McCormick were so rarely seen on their home stage. World War II put a temporary moratorium on foreign tours, but in the latter half of the century the company has toured extensively, playing frequently in Britain, and further afield in Australia,

Arthur Shields as Christopher Mahon in the 1925 production of The Playboy of the Western World *by J. M. Synge.*

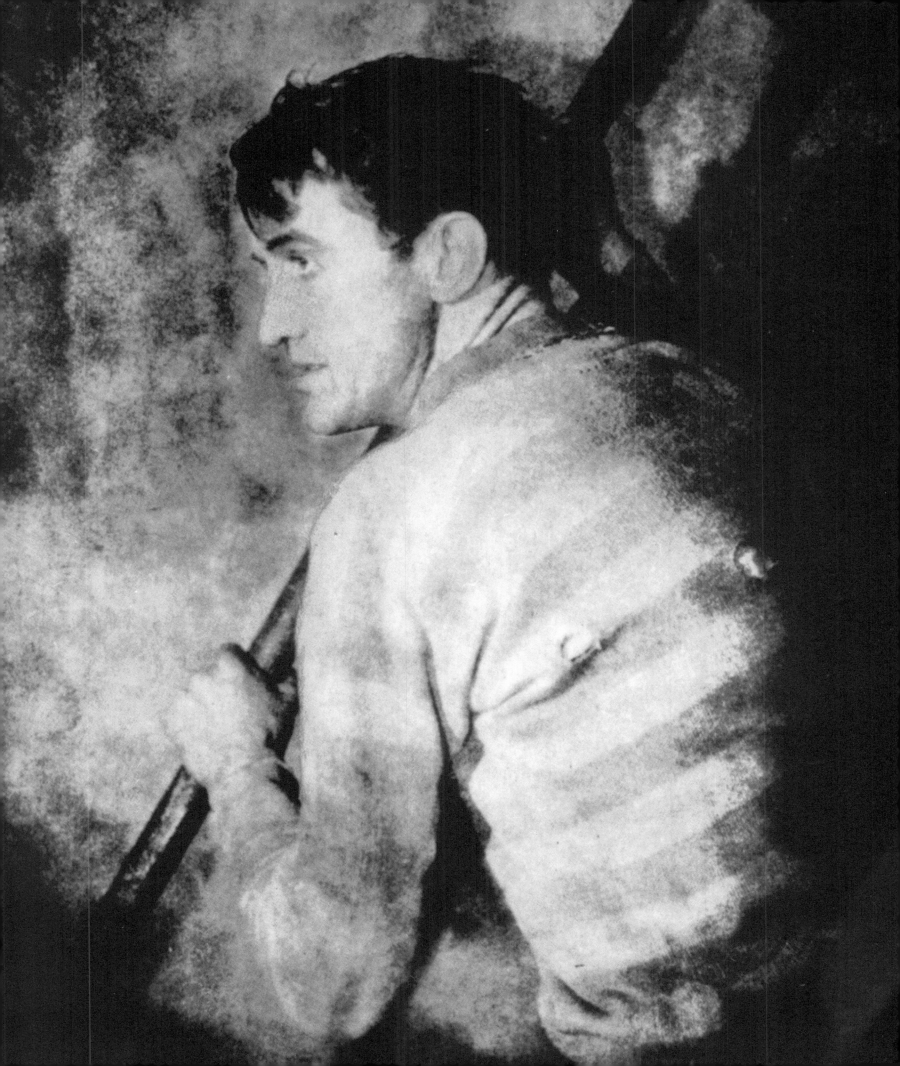

Belgium, Finland, France, Italy, Japan, Russia, Spain and the United States. The company has played to great acclaim, in plays from the early repertoire and more contemporary work by Irish writers including Brian Friel, John B. Keane, Tom Kilroy, Hugh Leonard, Frank McGuinness, Tom MacIntyre and Eugene O'Brien.

Courting Controversy

Few of the plays that later commentators would describe as great, plays that would be compared with those of leading dramatists in other countries, made their initial appearance without controversy of some kind. The first to cause a stir was Synge's exuberant comedy *The Playboy of the Western World* produced in 1907. With its exposition of mendacity and sexual jealousy and its gallous tale of parricide, *The Playboy* so inflamed sections of the audience that police had to be called to quell the disturbances. The same thing occurred in 1926 when Sean O'Casey's tragic satire, *The Plough and the Stars*, set at the time of the Easter Rising only ten years earlier, was found irredeemably shocking by those who could neither understand nor countenance what they saw as the dramatist's mocking view of a heroic revolution. These major plays quickly found their way onto the

Stephen Brennan, Colm Meaney, Fintan McKeown, Gabriel Byrne and Sean Lawlor in the 1979 production of Hatchet *by Heno Magee.*

PHOTO: FERGUS BOURKE

international stage, where they remain masterpieces of twentieth century western drama.

Views of a Free State

While Synge and O'Casey represent the apogee of the Abbey's early achievement, the playwrights whose works were performed throughout the nineteen-thirties and forties merit reassessment. Playwrights such as Paul Vincent Carroll, Louis D'Alton, Brinsley MacNamara and George Shiels brought a highly idiosyncratic interpretation of the Ireland of the Free State to the stage. Of these only Denis Johnston has received proper recognition in recent years. There is no doubt that his *The Moon in the Yellow River* was a milestone in the Abbey's creative journey, but he is also remembered for important contributions to other theatres and for his incomparable works of prose.

Making Space

Yeats recognized the need for a small intimate space for the performance of more poetic drama. A 101 seat experimental theatre was created out of two handsome Georgian reception rooms. It opened in 1927 and was named The Peacock after its exotic interior decoration. The buildings that comprised the Abbey and the Peacock were destroyed by fire in 1951. It

was decided to replace them with an entirely new theatre complex, designed by Michael Scott & Partners. This is largely what is to be seen today, and both theatres, as well as the company which inhabits them, are generally referred to collectively as 'the Abbey'.

Exile

After the fire, the Abbey company found a temporary home at the Queen's Theatre, across the river on Pearse Street. Some critics chose to see the fire as 'a cremation' and this period is usually regarded as one of exile in a Babylonian wilderness presided over by the managing director Ernest Blythe cast in the role of Nebuchadnezzar. Certainly the necessity of filling a much larger house by means of productions of lighter and supposedly more popular plays made for unadventurous programming. However, the period did see the production of early work by John B. Keane, Brian Friel and Hugh Leonard, as well as plays that confronted accepted notions of Irish history and contemporary society, among them James Plunkett's *The Risen People*, Denis Johnston's *The Scythe and the Sunset*, M.J. Molloy's *The Wood of the Whispering* and Seamus Byrne's *Design for a Headstone*. Literary critics were dismissive of John McCann's series of breezy comedies of Dublin life such

*Cyril Cusack,
and Philip O'Flynn in
the 1978 production of*
You Never Can Tell
by G.B. Shaw.

PHOTO: FERGUS BOURKE

as *Early and Often, Give Me A Bed Of Roses* and *It Can't Go On Forever*, the simple response was that without their commercial success the company would have collapsed.

Blythe's Spirit

Over the years, the Abbey has been reprimanded for its choice and non-choice of productions. The Abbey is constitutionally devoted to encouraging untried authors and takes risks as a matter of course. Too often do critics expect a first play to be a masterpiece, unfairly castigating writer and theatre if this is not so. They conveniently forget that Shakespeare, Molière and Miller all built gradually towards pre-eminence. The converse is also true, when the Abbey is castigated for 'snatching all the good new plays'. This is a no-win situation, and one hopes the Abbey will always regard it with forebearance.

The Abbey has also been condemned for failure to recognise new plays of unusual and undeniable significance. The nasty word is 'rejection'. This is part and parcel of a writer's life. O'Casey had plays turned down even after the success of *Plough*. Ernest Blythe, managing director from 1941 to 1967, has the distinction of penning the rejection letter to Brendan Behan, turning down his outstanding theatrical achievement *The Quare Fellow*. He also turned down Tom Murphy's

Scene from the 1994 production of Observe the Sons of Ulster Marching towards the Somme *by Frank McGuinness.*

PHOTO: AMELIA STEIN

ground-breaking *A Whistle in the Dark*, a play set in an Irish working-class ghetto in the English midlands, on the grounds that the kind of Irish people depicted did not exist. Thankfully, these plays found a receptive home with other managements. News of decisions of this kind did not enhance the Abbey's reputation as a 'literary' theatre. Indeed, during the early 1960s, plays such as Brian Friel's *Philadelphia, Here I Come!* or Eugene McCabe's *King of the Castle* were not written for the Abbey. Blythe was not alone in these decisions and the reading committee of the theatre, together with his fellow directors must shoulder some of this responsibility.

Much blame for the Abbey's mid-century doldrums has been unfairly laid at the tomb of Ernest Blythe. A reassessment of his role is long overdue. It was he, when Minister for Finance in the earliest Free State government, who arranged for the Abbey to benefit from an annual subsidy from central funds, the first theatre in the English-speaking world to be officially supported in this way. And had it not been for Blythe's untiring work as fundraiser when he was no longer part of government the new theatre would not have been built during the hungry 1950s.

A Growing Repertoire

What is curious and refreshing is that in spite of some embarrassing rejections the Abbey has consistently revisited earlier decisions, so that fine plays that did not initially find favour have later been incorporated into the repertoire. This, it is fair to add, has never been done in a spirit of self-condemnation, but simply because at some moment or other a producer or artistic director has felt moved to take such a play from the shelf and has been challenged by its special merits. Thus, rejected scripts like Keane's *Sive* have, in a strange way, become 'Abbey plays' in the public mind; and such is the manner in which the company has absorbed work originally seen elsewhere in the normal course of events, plays like Leonard's *Da* or Friel's *Translations*, it would be correct to say that the Abbey has taken unto itself the role of perpetuator of the whole canon of modern Irish dramatic literature.

A Writer's Theatre

The Abbey honours the precepts of its founders in its work with new and emerging playwrights. No other nation of comparable size and population presents as much provocative drama each year as does Ireland. This is

John Kavanagh as Drumm in the 2000 production of A Life *by Hugh Leonard.*

PHOTO: PAUL McCARTHY

principally due to the Abbey which has created an ethos of productivity that now extends far outside its own walls. Over its first century, the theatre has premiered no less than 725 new works on the stage. One manifestation of the theatre's current creativity is the way in which the work of dramatists of three generations is seen together on its stages. Brian Friel, Tom Kilroy, Hugh Leonard and Tom Murphy continue to write demanding work for the Abbey and for other theatres. Murphy's particular contribution to Ireland's dramatic heritage was saluted in 2001 with new productions of six of his most singular plays. Plays by the middle generation, led by Bernard Farrell with his mordant socially observant comedies of contemporary life, are presented side by side with those of younger playwrights, from Sebastian Barry's extraordinarily sensitive evocations of willfully forgotten people, places and times in Ireland to Marina Carr's explosive fusion of contemporary domestic concerns with terrifying primal rites.

Christopher Fitz-Simon
Author of The Abbey Theatre.
Ireland's National Theatre: The First 100 Years.

Maureen Toal, Eileen Colgan and Máire Ní Ghráinne in the 1979 production of Petticoat Loose *by M. J. Molloy.*

PHOTO: FERGUS BOURKE

January

JANUARY FIRST

1976, *Misé le Meas* by Eamon Kelly, Fergus Linehan, Tomás Mac Anna, Liam O'Ceallaigh, Eoghan O'Tuairisc - **Abbey Premiere.**

JANUARY SECOND

4 | 25 | 26 | 27 | 28 | 29 | 30 | 31

1991, *Danny, the Witch and the Gobbin* by Alan Cullen - **Abbey Premiere.**

Kate Duchene, Liz Kettle and Chris McHallem in the 2001 production of Iphigenia at Aulis *translated by Don Taylor, after Euripides.*

PHOTO: PAT REDMOND

JANUARY FOURTH

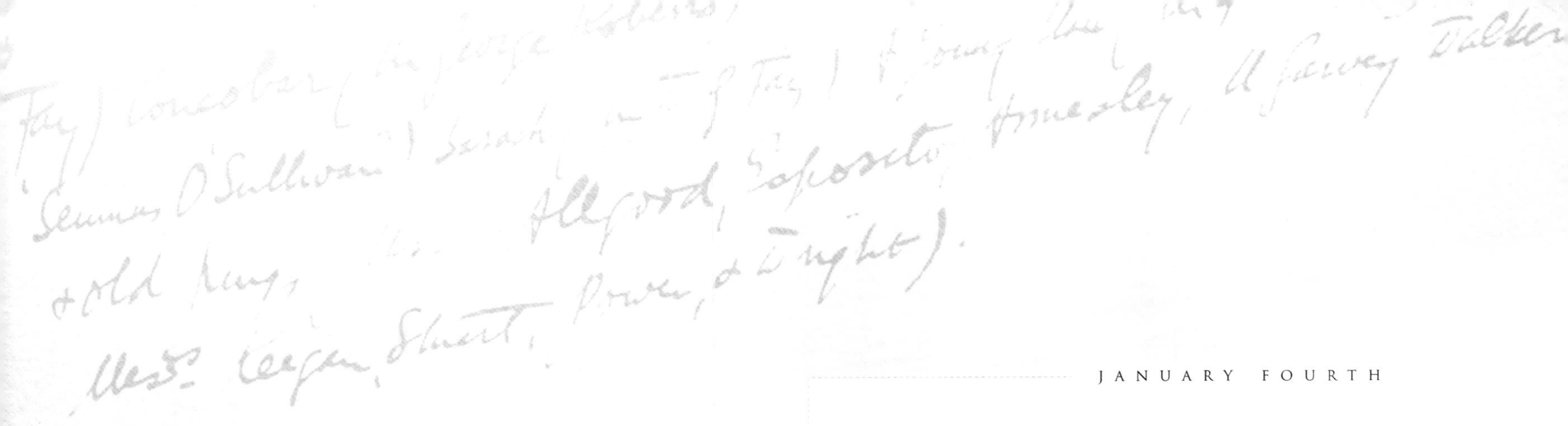

1916, ***Fraternity*** by Bernard Duffy - World Premiere.

JANUARY THIRD

JANUARY FIFTH

1911, ***A Nativity Play*** by Douglas Hyde and Lady Gregory - World Premiere.

Des Cave as Oedipus in the
1973 production of
King Oedipus *by*
W.B. Yeats, after Sophocles.

PHOTO: FERGUS BOURKE

J A N U A R Y   S I X T H

1921, *Bedmates* by George Shiels - World Premiere.

J A N U A R Y   S E V E N T H

1945, *An t-Ubhall Óir* translated by Liam Ó Briain,
after Lady Gregory - **Abbey Premiere.**

*Stephen Brennan,
Dearbhla Molloy, Garrett
Keogh and Ingrid Craigie
in the 1979 World Premiere
of* A Life *by Hugh
Leonard.*

PHOTO: FERGUS BOURKE

JANUARY EIGHT

1918, *Spring* by T. C. Murray - World Premiere.

JANUARY NINTH

1923, *The Long Road to Garranbraher*, by J. B. Mac Carthy
- World Premiere.

JANUARY TENTH

1985, *Candide '85* adapted by Eamon Morrissey
and Tomás Mac Anna, after Voltaire - World Premiere.

*Des Cave and Anita
Reeves in the 2003
production of* She
Stoops to Conquer
by Oliver Goldsmith.

PHOTO: TOM LAWLOR

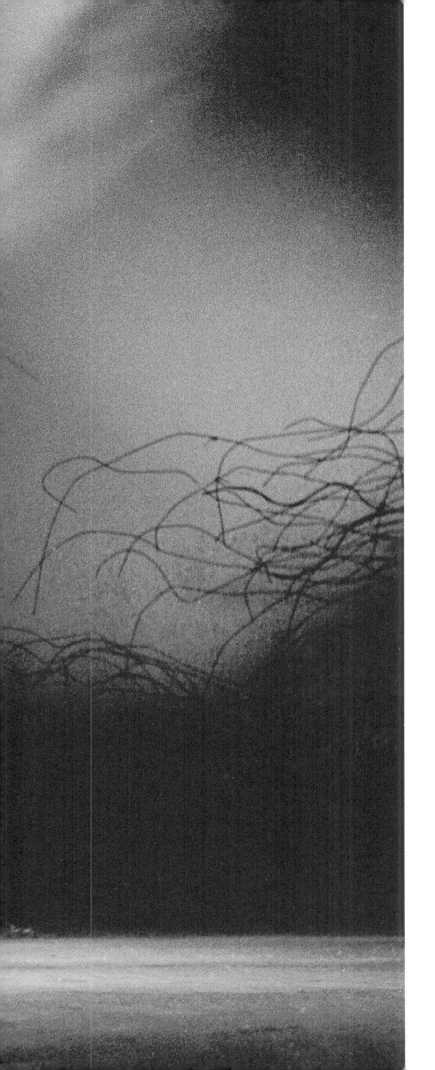

JANUARY ELEVENTH

1971, *The Homecoming* by Harold Pinter - **Abbey Premiere.**

JANUARY TWELFTH

1911, *The Deliverer* by Lady Gregory - World Premiere.

Ruth McCabe and
Brendan Gleeson in the
1989 production of
King of the Castle *by*
Eugene Mc Cabe.

PHOTO: FERGUS BOURKE

ABBEY THEATRE.

OPENING PERFORMANCES

TUESDAY, 27TH DEC.

TO

TUESDAY, 3RD JAN.

Printed by An Cló-Cumann, Limited, Gaelic Printers, Great Strand street, Dublin.

1910, *Deirdre Of The Sorrows* by J. M. Synge - World Premiere.

1974, *The Resistable Rise of Arturo Ui* by Bertolt Brecht - **Abbey Premiere.**

1968, *The Last Eleven* by Jack White - World Premiere.

1979, *Portrait of a Madonna* by Tennessee Williams - **Abbey Premiere.**

JANUARY SEVENTEENTH

1973, *The School For Scandal* by Richard B. Sheridan, **Abbey Premiere.**

JANUARY EIGHTEENTH

*Des Cave and Donal
McCann in the
1980 production of
The Shadow of a
Gunman by
Sean O'Casey.*

PHOTO: FERGUS BOURKE

1957, *A Leap in the Dark* by Hugh Leonard - World Premiere.

1906, *Riders to the Sea* by J. M. Synge - **Abbey Premiere.**

Ray McAnally and Gerard
McSorley in the
1972 production of
Philadelphia, Here I Come!
by Brian Friel.

PHOTO: FERGUS BOURKE

JANUARY TWENTY SECOND

1917, *Crusaders* by J. B. Mac Carthy - World Premiere.

JANUARY TWENTY THIRD

1956, *The Big Birthday* by Hugh Leonard - World Premiere.

*Donal McCann as
Terry in the 1993
production of
Wonderful Tennessee
by Brian Friel.*

PHOTO: TOM LAWLOR

JANUARY TWENTY FOURTH

2001, *Eden* by Eugene O'Brien - World Premiere.

JANUARY TWENTY SIXTH

1907, *The Playboy of the Western World* by J. M. Synge - World Premiere.

JANUARY TWENTY FIFTH

1937, *Shadow and Substance* by Paul Vincent Carroll - World Premiere.

JANUARY TWENTY SEVENTH

1915, *By Word of Mouth* by F. C. Moore and W. P. Flanagan - World Premiere.

ABBEY THEATRE
DUBLIN.

LESSEE - A. E. F. HORNIMAN

IRISH PLAYS

PRESENTED BY THE

NATIONAL THEATRE SOCIETY.

THURSDAY, NOV. 7TH, '07
FOR THREE NIGHTS.
MATINEE, SATURDAY, NOVEMBER 9th, at 2.30.

HYACINTH HALVEY
A Comedy in One Act, by Lady Gregory.

Hyacinth Halvey	F. J. Fay	Sergeant Carden	J. A. O'Rourke
James Quirke	W. G. Fay	Mrs. Delane	Sara Allgood
Fardy Farrell	Arthur Sinclair	Miss Joyce	Brigit O'Dempsey

Scene—Outside the Post Office at the Town of Cloon.

THE HOUR GLASS
A Morality in One Act, by W. B. YEATS

The Wise Man	Ernest Vaughan	His Pupils	Arthur Sinclair,
Bridget, his wife	Maire O'Neill		J. A. O'Rourke, & J. M. Kerrigan
His Children	Michael Dunne and John Dunne	The Angel	Sara Allgood
		The Fool	F. J. Fay

THE LAND
A Play in Three Acts, by PADRAIC COLM. (By Arrangement.)

Murtagh Cosgar, a farmer	W. G. Fay	Ellen, his daughter	Brigit O'Dempsey
Matt, his son	J. M. Kerrigan	A Farmer, a Shopkeeper,	T. J. Fox, J. A. O'Rourke,
Sally, his daughter	Maire O'Neill	and a County Councillor	and Ernest Vaughan.
Martin Douras	F. J. Fay	A Boy	J. A. O'Rourke
Cornelius, his son	Arthur Sinclair	A Girl	Sara Allgood

The Scene is laid in the Irish Midlands, present time. The action is contemporary with the stage presentation.

Orchestra - Under the Direction of G. R. HILLIS

General Manager and Stage Director
Business Manager
Assistant Stage Manager

For the National
Theatre Society, Ltd.

W. G. FAY
ERNEST VAUGHAN
J. A. O'ROURKE

STALLS, 3s.; BALCONY RESERVED, 2s.; FRONT PIT, 1s.; BACK PIT, 6d.

CORRIGAN & WILSON, Printers, 13 Sackville Place, Dublin.

JANUARY TWENTY EIGHT

1998, *The Wake* by Tom Murphy - World Premiere.

JANUARY TWENTY NINTH

1940, *The Spanish Soldier* by Louis D'Alton - World Premiere.

*Scene from the
1977 production of*
The Old Lady Says No!
by Denis Johnston.

PHOTO: FERGUS BOURKE

JANUARY THIRTIETH

1975, *Purple Dust* by Sean O'Casey - **Abbey Premiere.**

JANUARY THIRTY FIRST

1980, **The Field** by John B. Keane - **Abbey Premiere.**

*Stephen Brennan, John
Molloy, Clive Geraghty,
Ingrid Craigie and
Eileen Colgan in the
1977 production of
Talbot's Box by
Thomas Kilroy.*

PHOTO: FERGUS BOURKE

February

1 | 2 | 3 | 4 | 5 | 6 | 7 | 8 | 9 | 10 | 11 | 12 | 13 | 14 | 15 | 16 | 17 | 18 | 19 | 20 | 21 | 22 | 2

FEBRUARY FIRST

2002, *Hinterland* by Sebastian Barry - **Abbey Premiere.**

FEBRUARY SECOND

1988, *Exit Entrance* by Aidan Mathews - World Premiere.

*Eamon Morrissey as
Don Gallant in the 2000
production of* Barbaric
Comedies *in a new version
by Frank McGuinness, after
Ramón María del Valle-Inclán.*

PHOTO: DOUGLAS ROBERTSON

4 | 25 | 26 | 27 | 28 | 29

1905, *The Well of the Saints* by J. M. Synge -World Premiere.

1981, *Footfalls* by Samuel Beckett - **Abbey Premiere.**

1987, *Dialann Ocrais*, Peter Sheridan - **Abbey Premiere.**

Donal McCann as Frank in the 1980 Abbey Premiere of Faith Healer by Brian Friel.

PHOTO: FERGUS BOURKE

1933, *Drama at Inish* by Lennox Robinson - World Premiere.

1996, *The Invisible Mending Company* by Philip Davison - World Premiere.

*Scene from the 1987
production of
Madigan's Lock by
Hugh Leonard.*

PHOTO: FERGUS BOURKE

1926, *The Plough and the Stars* by Sean O'Casey - World Premiere.

1976, *The Birthday Party* by Harold Pinter - **Abbey Premiere.**

1920, *The Devil's Disciple* by G. B. Shaw - **Abbey Premiere.**

Excerpt from the diaries of Joseph Holloway.

COURTESY OF THE NATIONAL LIBRARY OF IRELAND

1946, *Mungo's Mansions* by Walter Macken - World Premiere.

FEBRUARY TWELFTH

1997, *In a Little World of Our Own* by Gary Mitchell - World Premiere.

Dearbhla Molloy and
Gerard Mc Sorley in
the 1991 production of
Dancing at Lughnasa
by Brian Friel.

PHOTO: FERGUS BOURKE

IRISH NATIONAL FORESTERS

Branch:—BROS. PEARSE, No. 1,114

GRAND CONCERT

WILL BE GIVEN IN THE

ABBEY THEATRE

Under the Auspices of the above

On Sunday, 13th May, '28

When the following Pick of Dublin's Talent will appear:

Miss L. MOONEY'S No. 1 & 2 TROUPES

In A Classical Acrobatic and Laughable Dutch Dancing Act

Humorists	Vocalists	Dancers
GEORGE BLACK	FRED DUNNE	MURTAGH, McKENNA & CONNOLLY Just Three Dancers
MIKE WHELAN	J. J. MANNING	GEORGE LEONARD Ireland's Champion Boy Dancer
PAT WHELAN	W. MURPHY	MISS DOLLY MOONEY In Ashcroft's Song and Dance
JOSEPH CHEEVERS	M. DUNLEAVY	MISS K. BRENNAN Tailteann Champion

ENTERTAINERS

MISS JOSIE McMAHON	TWO DUBLIN BOYS
MIKE KEOGH	THE MUSICAL FIVE

THE BOHEMIAN ENTERTAINERS

MACKEN & BRACKEN

THE WHITE BLACKBIRDS   DISPELLERS OF GLOOM

GEORGE McNALLY

(THAT'S ALL)

ADMISSION - - - 1s., 2s. & 3s.

Doors open at 7 p.m.; commencing at 7.30 p.m.   BOOKING AT ABBEY THEATRE OFFICE

O'KEEFFE, Printer, Capel Street, Dublin.

1908, *The Piper*, Norreys Connell - World Premiere.

1938, *A Spot In The Sun* by T. C. Murray - World Premiere.

1990, *Tagann Godot* by Alan Titley - World Premiere.

1911, *The Land of Heart's Desire* by W. B. Yeats - **Abbey Premiere.**

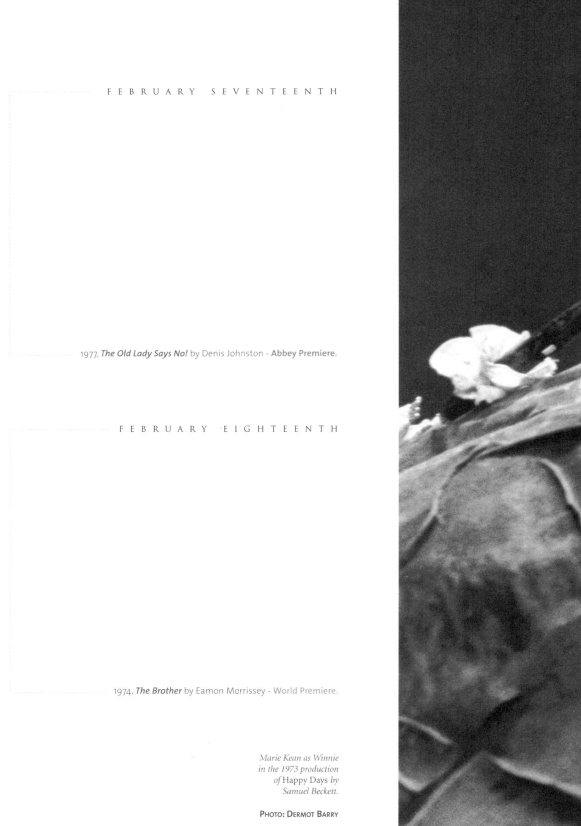

1977, *The Old Lady Says No!* by Denis Johnston - **Abbey Premiere.**

1974, *The Brother* by Eamon Morrissey - World Premiere.

*Marie Kean as Winnie
in the 1973 production
of* Happy Days *by
Samuel Beckett.*

PHOTO: DERMOT BARRY

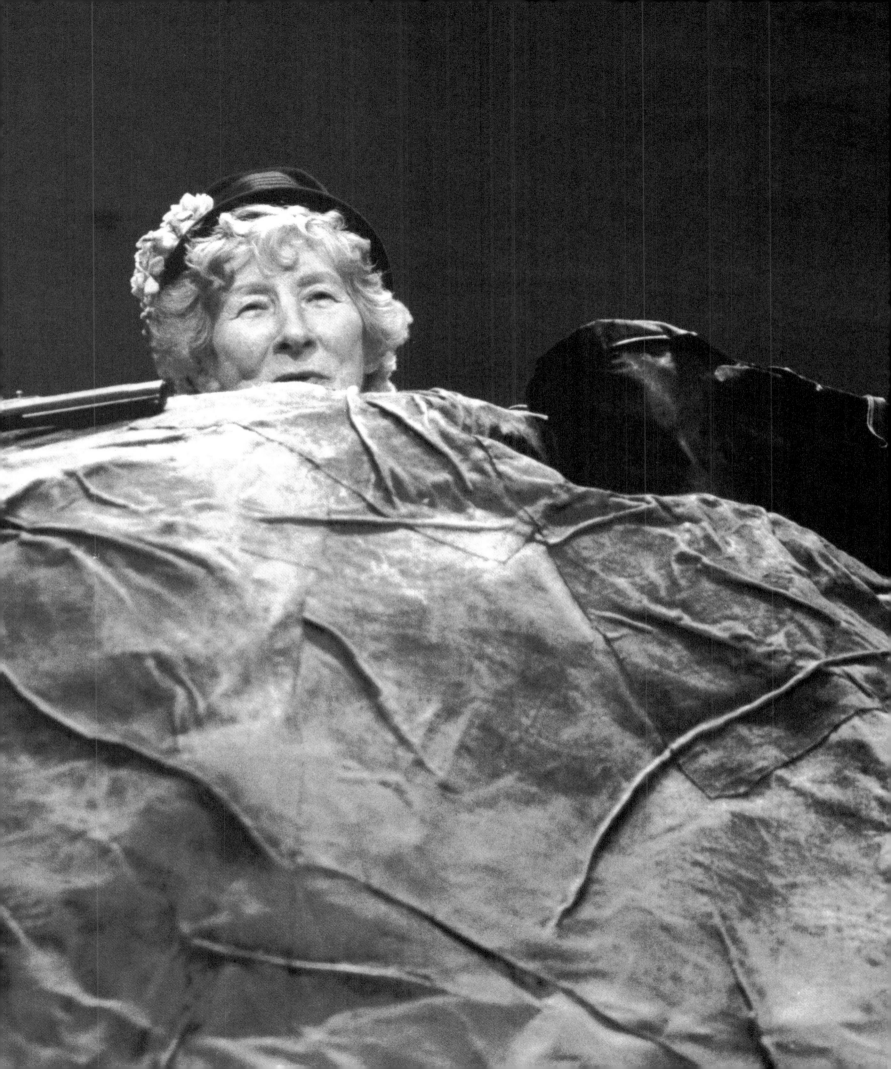

1973, *The Freedom of the City* by Brian Friel - World Premiere.

FEBRUARY NINETEENTH

FEBRUARY TWENTY FIRST

1906, *Hyacinth Halvey* by Lady Gregory - World Premiere.

1973, *Exiles* by James Joyce - **Abbey Premiere.**

John Molloy as
Matt Talbot in the
1977 production of
Talbot's Box by
Thomas Kilroy.

PHOTO: FERGUS BOURKE

FEBRUARY TWENTY SECOND

1954, *John Courtney* by John Malone - World Premiere.

FEBRUARY TWENTY THIRD

1907, *Sheep's Milk on the Boil* by Tom MacIntyre - World Premiere.

The Abbey Theatre Company of the late 1920's. Back row: L-R Unknown, M.J. Dolan, Maureen Delany, P.J. Carolan, Eileen Crowe and Denis O'Dea. Front row: L-R Arthur Shields, May Craig, F.J. Mc Cormick, Shelah Richards, Barry Fitzgerald and Frolie Mulhern.

Photo: National Theatre Archives

1921, *The Revolutionist* by Terence Mac Swiney - World Premiere.

1998, *Twenty Grand* by Declan Hughes - World Premiere.

1917, *Man and Superman* by G. B. Shaw - **Abbey Premiere.**

1987, *Dance for your Daddy* by Tom Mac Intyre - World Premiere.

Excerpt from the diaries of Joseph Holloway.

COURTESY OF THE NATIONAL LIBRARY OF IRELAND

... Harold's Cross Parochial Hall, Kenilworth Road, etc. Second

... Rev John & Jennings.

... frantic night into a cold penetrating fog accompanied me
... and from St Matthews Parochial Hall Irishtown then
... Flint gave a recital of Schumann's Songs accompanied by
... Allen before an appreciative but small audience. The Rev
... olin gave a short sketch of the composer's life between these
... three combined in giving those present an intellectual treat.
... Flint sang of selections in all. Sixteen of these were comprised in
... Dichterliebe cycle of love songs which he interpreted with artistic
... ... And employed the tongue (German) in which they were writ-
... He sang the other three, oz., Devotion, Folk Song, & the two Grena-
... diers — to English words. Each of his selections won applause. Miss Allen
... at the piano was excellent & her solo much appreciated. The Rev S.
... Carolin made his part-accompaniment & homely ...
... cluded about 25 to 10, & I married away with the rest of the audience
... without stealing to her Flint ...
... roaring fire made the audience feel quite cheery.
... 26 Saturday. Abbey Theatre. First performance of Synge's play, The Playboy

FEBRUARY TWENTY EIGHT

1938, **Moses' Rock** by Frank O'Connor and Hugh Hunt - World Premiere.

FEBRUARY TWENTY NINTH

1916, **The Patriot** by Maeve O'Callaghan - World Premiere.

Kevin McHugh
(foreground) and
Colm Meaney in the 1980
production of The Closed
Door *by J. Graham Reid.*

PHOTO: FERGUS BOURKE

*Full theatre shot of the Abbey with stage set for the
2002 production of* The Plough and the Stars *by
Sean O'Casey, designed by Francis O'Connor.*

PHOTO: TOM LAWLOR

March

1 | 2 | 3 | 4 | 5 | 6 | 7 | 8 | 9 | 10 | 11 | 12 | 13 | 14 | 15 | 16 | 17 | 18 | 19 | 20 | 21 | 22 | 2

1971, *The Devil at Work* by Constantine Fitzgibbon - World Premiere.

MARCH SECOND

4 | 2 5 | 2 6 | 2 7 | 2 8 | 2 9 | 3 0 | 3 1

1993, *The Comedy of Errors* by William Shakespeare - **Abbey Premiere.**

Bosco Hogan as
W.B. Yeats in the 1988
production of
I Am of Ireland
by Edward Callan.

PHOTO: FERGUS BOURKE

1976, *Lovers* by Brian Friel - **Abbey Premiere.**

1924, *Juno and the Paycock* by Sean O'Casey - World Premiere.

1985, *Baglady* by Frank Mc Guinness - World Premiere.

Brenda Fricker,
Eamon Kelly and
Maura O'Sullivan
in the 1988 production
of Big Maggie *by*
John B. Keane.

PHOTO: FERGUS BOURKE

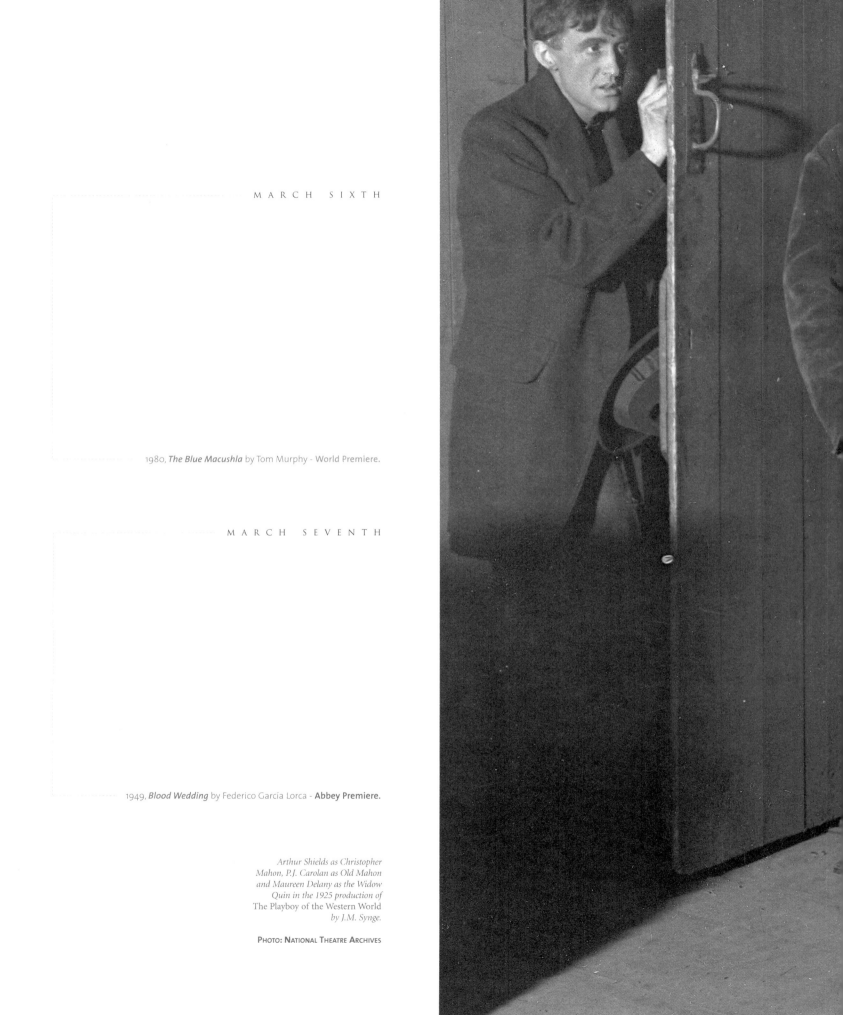

MARCH SIXTH

1980, *The Blue Macushla* by Tom Murphy - World Premiere.

MARCH SEVENTH

1949, *Blood Wedding* by Federico Garcia Lorca - **Abbey Premiere.**

*Arthur Shields as Christopher
Mahon, P.J. Carolan as Old Mahon
and Maureen Delany as the Widow
Quin in the 1925 production of
The Playboy of the Western World
by J.M. Synge.*

PHOTO: NATIONAL THEATRE ARCHIVES

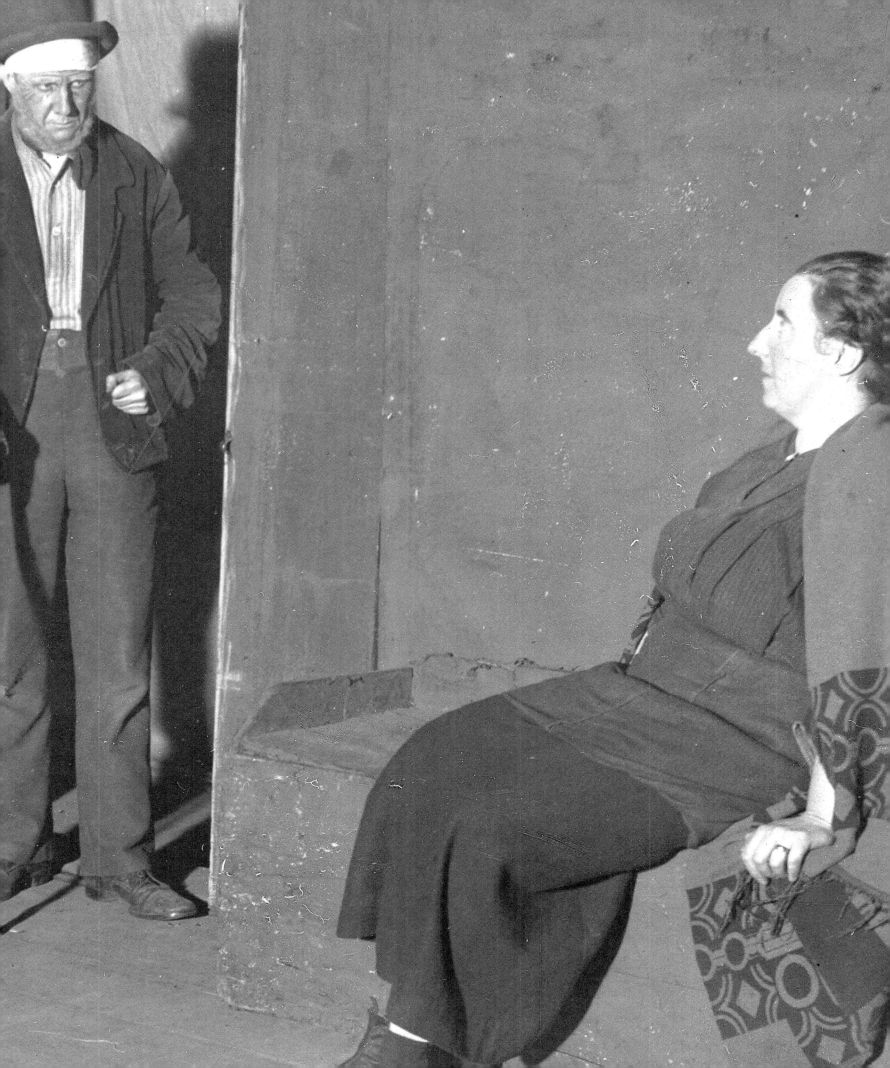

1979, *Aristocrats* by Brian Friel - World Premiere.

1907, *The Rising of the Moon* by Lady Gregory - World Premiere.

1999, *Love In The Title* by Hugh Leonard - World Premiere.

ABBEY THEATRE

ONE NIGHT ONLY.

Sunday, 3rd February, 1929, at 8 o'c.

ISRAEL

Dublin — **IN THE** — **Jewish**

Dramatic **KITCHEN** **Society**

By NOAH ELSTEIN.

"A Jewish *JUNO AND THE PAYCOCK* . . . The Play is a Slice of Real Life."—*Manchester Guardian.*

Play Produced by GABRIEL FALLON.

Booking at Theatre. **Usual Abbey Prices.**

CORRIGAN & WILSON, LTD., Printers, 13 Sackville Place, Dublin

1919, *The Rebellion in Ballycullen* by Brinsley Mac Namara - World Premiere.

1997, *Give me your answer, do!* by Brian Friel - World Premiere.

Niall O'Brien, Stephen Rea and Kate Flynn in the 1979 World Premiere of Aristocrats by Brian Friel.

PHOTO: FERGUS BOURKE

1993, *Someone Who'll Watch Over Me* by Frank Mc Guinness - **Abbey Premiere.**

1979, *I do not like thee, Dr. Fell* by Bernard Farrell - World Premiere.

1972, *Richard's Cork Leg* by Brendan Behan - World Premiere.

1907, *Interior* by Maurice Maeterlinck - **Abbey Premiere.**

Kate Duchene, Stella Feehily,
Liz Kettle and Pauline Hutton
as Iphigenia (foreground) in
the 2001 production of
Iphigenia at Aulis *translated by*
Don Taylor, after Euripides.

PHOTO: PAT REDMOND

MARCH SEVENTEENTH

1958, *Look In The Looking-Glass* by Walter Macken - World Premiere.

MARCH EIGHTEENTH

1968, *The Saint and Mary Kate* adapted by Mary Manning,
after Frank O'Connor - World Premiere.

Catherine Walsh as
Lizzie Maher in the
2001 production of
Blackwater Angel *by*
Jim Nolan.

PHOTO: PAUL MCCARTHY

ABBEY
THEATRE

Proprietors · THE NATIONAL THEATRE SOCIETY, LTD.
Directors · LENNOX ROBINSON, WALTER STARKIE, DR. RICHARD HAYES
ERNEST BLYTHE, F. R. HIGGINS
Secretary · ERIC GORMAN

MONDAY, 31ST JULY

And Following Nights at 8.15.   Doors Open at 7.45

FIRST PRODUCTION OF

ILLUMINATION

A PLAY IN TWO ACTS, BY T. C. MURRAY

IN THE TRAIN

A PLAY IN ONE ACT FROM THE SHORT STORY BY FRANK O'CONNOR
DRAMATISED BY HUGH HUNT

PRICES :

Stalls, 5/- & 3/-;   Balcony, 2/6 & 1/-;   Pit, 2/- & 1/6
(ALL SEATS CAN BE RESERVED)

BOX OFFICE 10.30 TO 6   'PHONE 44505

Corrigan & Wilson, Ltd., 13 Sackville Place, Dublin.

1972, *The White House* by Tom Murphy - World Premiere.

1908, *The Piedish* by George Fitzmaurice - World Premiere.

1968, *Famine* by Tom Murphy - World Premiere.

MARCH TWENTY SECOND

1922, *A Doll's House* translated by R. Farquharson Sharp, after Henrik Ibsen - **Abbey Premiere.**

MARCH TWENTY THIRD

1970, *At Swim-Two-Birds* adapted by Audrey Welch, after Flann O'Brien - **Abbey Premiere.**

Scene from the 1985 production of Observe the Sons of Ulster Marching towards the Somme *by Frank McGuinness.*

PHOTO: FERGUS BOURKE

MARCH TWENTY FOURTH

1977, *Living Quarters* by Brian Friel - World Premiere.

MARCH TWENTY SIXTH

1917, *The Doctor's Dilemma* by G. B. Shaw - **Abbey Premiere.**

MARCH TWENTY FIFTH

1991, *Ullaloo* by Marina Carr - World Premiere.

MARCH TWENTY SEVENTH

1996, *Portia Coughlan* by Marina Carr - World Premiere.

Portrait of Lady Gregory

LADY
GREGORY.

MARCH TWENTY EIGHT

2001, *Iphigenia at Aulis* translated by Don Taylor, after Euripides - **Abbey Premiere.**

MARCH TWENTY NINE

1954, *Twenty Years A-Wooing* by John McCann - World Premiere.

*Emma Colohan, Gina Moxley,
Stella Feehily, Kelly Campbell
and Liz Kettle in the
2001 production of* Iphigenia
at Aulis *translated by Don
Taylor, after Euripides.*

PHOTO: PAUL MCCARTHY

MARCH THIRTIETH

1911, *Mixed Marriage* by St. John Ervine - World Premiere.

MARCH THIRTY FIRST

1925, *Portrait* by Lennox Robinson - World Premiere.

Scene from the 1979 production of A Flea in Her Ear *adapted by Fergus Linehan, after Georges Feydeau.*

PHOTO: FERGUS BOURKE

April

1 | 2 | 3 | 4 | 5 | 6 | 7 | 8 | 9 | 10 | 11 | 12 | 13 | 14 | 15 | 16 | 17 | 18 | 19 | 20 | 21 | 22 |

APRIL FIRST

APRIL SECOND

| 25 | 26 | 27 | 28 | 29 | 30 |

Cathy Belton as Betty in the 2001 production of A Whistle in the Dark *by Tom Murphy.*

PHOTO: PAUL MCCARTHY

1942, *The Singer* by Padraig Pearse - **Abbey Premiere.**

1907, *The Poorhouse* by Lady Gregory and Douglas Hyde - World Premiere.

1937, *Alarm Among The Clerks* by Mervyn Wall - World Premiere.

*Eamon Morrissey
in the 1978 production
of* Faustus Kelly *by
Flann O'Brien.*

PHOTO: FERGUS BOURKE

APRIL SIXTH

1922, ***Ann Kavanagh*** by Dorothy Macardle - World Premiere.

APRIL SEVENTH

1983, ***The Midnight Door*** by Aodhan Madden - World Premiere.

*Colm Meaney, Bryan Murray, Clive Geraghty, Raymond Hardie,
Emmet Bergin, Niall O'Brien, Eamon Morrissey, John Kavanagh and
Robert Carlisle as the chorus in the 1973 production of* King Oedipus *by
W.B. Yeats, after Sophocles.*

PHOTO: FERGUS BOURKE

1976, *Desire Under the Elms* by Eugene O'Neill - **Abbey Premiere.**

1997, *Sour Grapes* by Michael Harding - World Premiere.

1901, *Made in China* by Mark O'Rowe - World Premiere.

Caricature of Lennox Robinson

Abbey Theatre
PATRIC[K]
LENNOX ROB[INSON]

Lennox Rob[inson]

APRIL ELEVENTH

2000, *Tree Houses* by Elizabeth Kuti - World Premiere.

APRIL TWELFTH

1923, *The Shadow of a Gunman* by Sean O'Casey - World Premiere.

*Philip O'Flynn as Kearns
and Cyril Cusack as Drumm
in the 1979 World Premiere
of* A Life *by Hugh Leonard.*

PHOTO: FERGUS BOURKE

ABBEY THEATRE

FOR ONE WEEK ONLY

COMMENCING MONDAY 1st. NOV. at 8 p.m.

DANNY CUMMINS

IN

DUBLIN LAUGHS AGAIN

WITH

THE HAPPY GANG

CECIL NASH	★	FRANK HOWARD
BILL BRADY	★	VAL FITZPATRICK
IMELDA SISTERS	★	PATRICIA O'KEEFFE
BRENDA DOYLE	★	ARTHUR MADDEN
DEREK COBBE & Co	★	The ROYALETTES

GUEST ARTISTES APPEARING INCLUDE:

MAUREEN POTTER ★ BUTCH MOORE ★ MRS. KENNEDY of CASTLEROSS ★ DICKIE ROCK ★ AND A HOST OF OTHERS

PAT KING & ORCHESTRA ★ FULL SUPPORTING CAST

CHOREOGRAPHY by ALICE DALGARNO   COSTUMES DESIGNED by BABS DELMONTE

POPULAR PRICES - BOOKING AT THEATRE

1936, *The Passing Day* by George Shiels - World Premiere.

2003, *The House of Bernarda Alba* translated by Sebastian Barry,
after Frederico García Lorca - World Premiere.

1909, *The Heather Field* by Edward Martyn - **Abbey Premiere.**

1949, *All Soul's Night* by Joseph Tomelty - World Premiere.

APRIL SEVENTEENTH

1989, *Una Pooka* by Michael Harding - World Premiere.

APRIL EIGHTEENTH

1989, *Shades of a Jelly Woman* by Peter Sheridan - **Abbey Premiere.**

*Patrick Leech as
Captain Brennan and
Aonghus Óg Mc Anally as
Lieutenant Langon in the
2002 production of*
The Plough and the Stars *by
Sean O'Casey.*

PHOTO: TOM LAWLOR

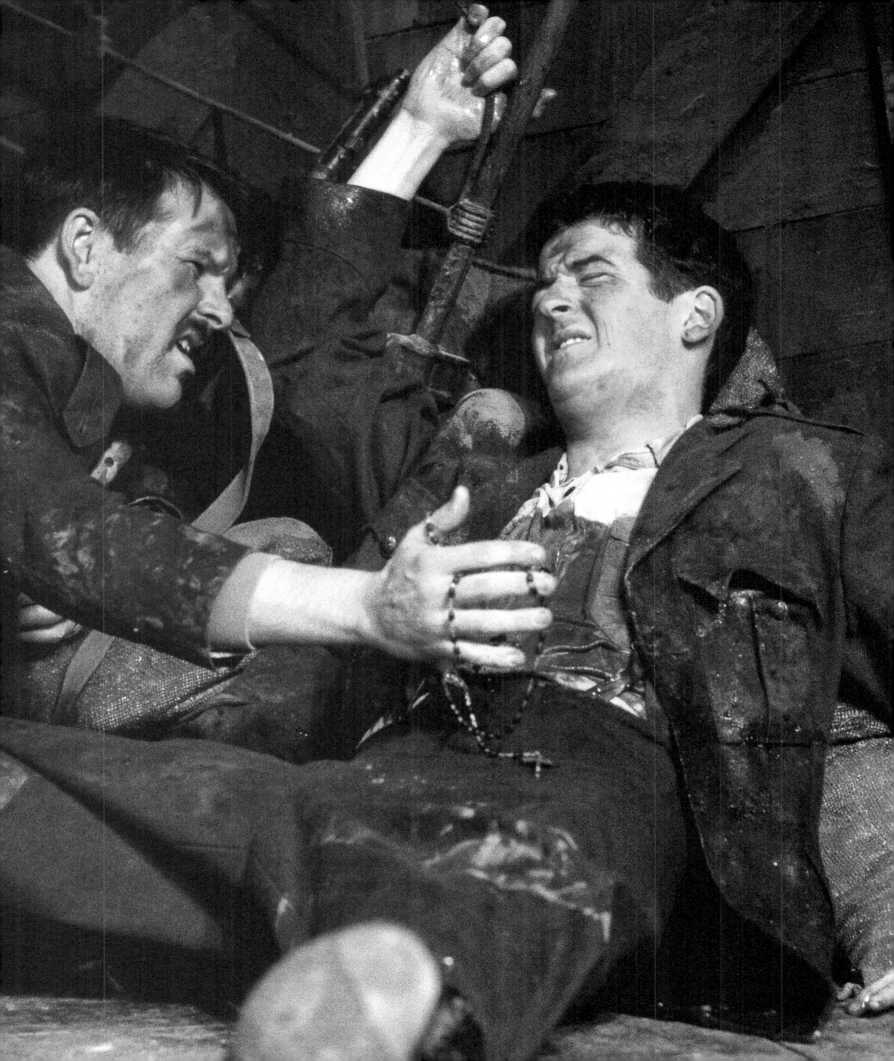

1978, *Hisself* by Pat Ingoldsby - World Premiere.

1993, *Hubert Murray's Widow* by Michael Harding - World Premiere.

1982, *The Hidden Curriculum* by J. Graham Reid - World Premiere.

Fiona Glascott as Mibs
in the 2000 production of
A Life by Hugh Leonard.

PHOTO: TOM LAWLOR

1957, *The Flying Wheel* by Donal Giltinan - World Premiere.

1992, *The Winter Thief* by Seán Mac Mathúna - World Premiere.

*Maura O'Sullivan, Maeve
Germaine and Eamon Kelly in
the 1989 production of
Big Maggie by John B. Keane.*

PHOTO: FERGUS BOURKE

APRIL TWENTY FOURTH

1990, *Dancing at Lughnasa* by Brian Friel - World Premiere.

APRIL TWENTY SIXTH

1971, *The Tinker's Wedding* by J. M. Synge - **Abbey Premiere.**

APRIL TWENTY FIFTH

2001, *Mann ist Mann* by Bertolt Brecht - **Abbey Premiere.**

APRIL TWENTY SEVENTH

1931, *The Moon in the Yellow River* by Denis Johnston - World Premiere.

Maureen Toal, John Kavanagh, Stephen Brennan, Colm Meaney, Philip O'Flynn in the 1978 production of Hatchet *by Heno Magee.*

PHOTO: FERGUS BOURKE

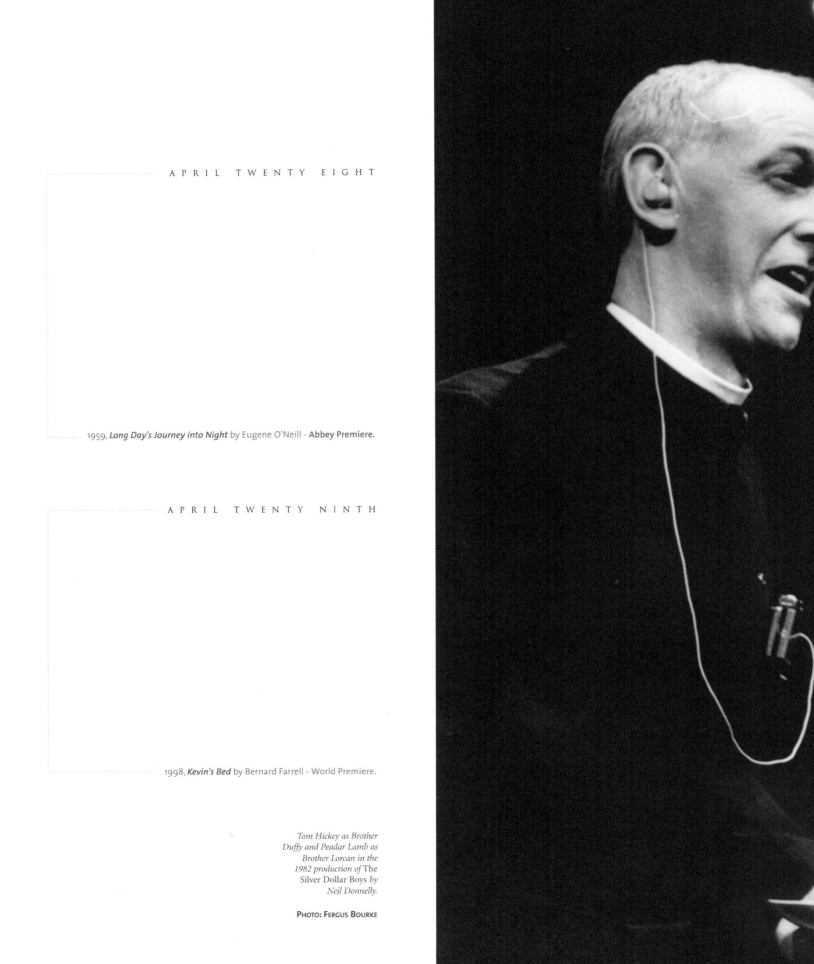

APRIL TWENTY EIGHT

1959, *Long Day's Journey into Night* by Eugene O'Neill - **Abbey Premiere.**

APRIL TWENTY NINTH

1998, *Kevin's Bed* by Bernard Farrell - **World Premiere.**

Tom Hickey as Brother
Duffy and Peadar Lamb as
Brother Lorcan in the
1982 production of The
Silver Dollar Boys *by*
Neil Donnelly.

PHOTO: FERGUS BOURKE

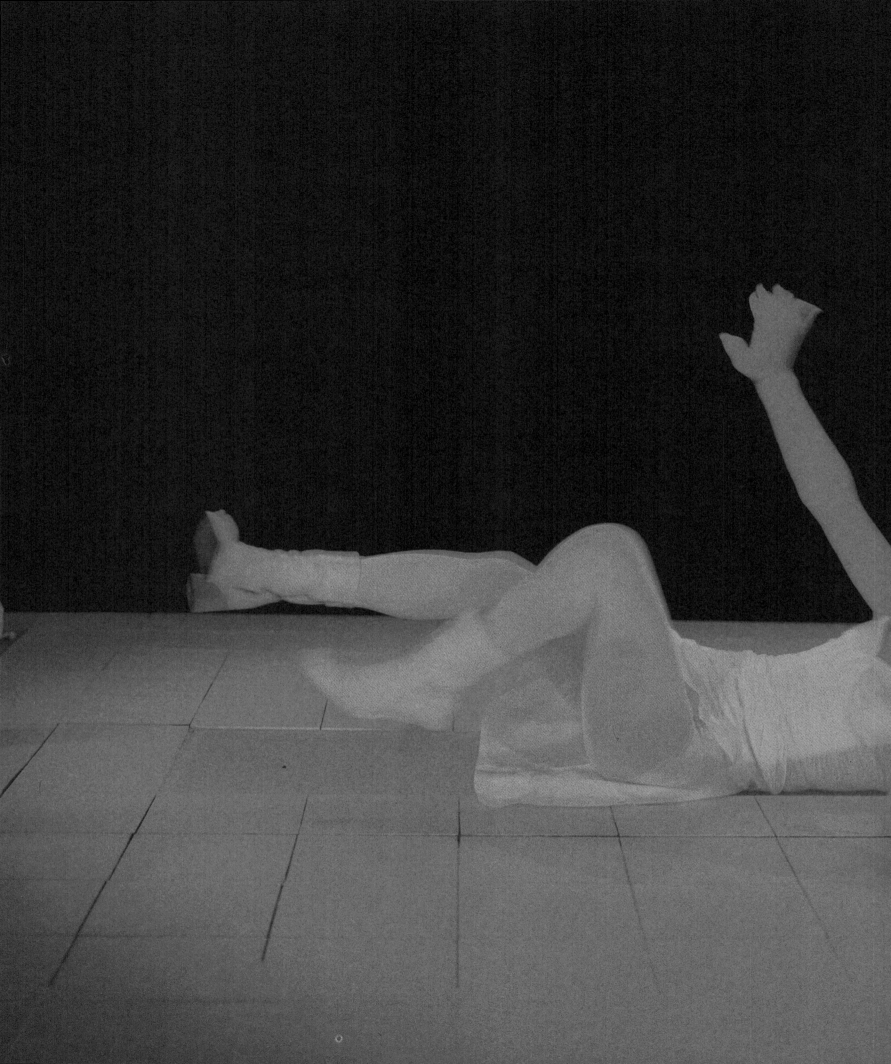

30th 1981, *Buried Child* by Sam Sheperd - **Abbey Premiere.**

*Olwen Fouéré in the
2001 co-production of*
Chair *by Operating
Theatre Company.
Peacock Partner
Production.*

PHOTO: AMELIA STEIN

May

1 | 2 | 3 | 4 | 5 | 6 | 7 | 8 | 9 | 10 | 11 | 12 | 13 | 14 | 15 | 16 | 17 | 18 | 19 | 20 | 21 | 22 |

4 | 25 | 26 | 27 | 28 | 29 | 30 | 31

*Máire O'Neill as Lady
Gregory in the 1987
production of* Lady G
by Caroline Swift.

PHOTO: FERGUS BOURKE

MAY FIRST

2002, *Communion* by Aidan Mathews - World Premiere.

MAY SECOND

1972, *Hatchet* by Heno Magee - World Premiere.

1920, *The Yellow Bittern* by Daniel Corkery - **Abbey Premiere.**

1972, *The Iceman Cometh* by Eugene O'Neill - **Abbey Premiere.**

1910, *Thomas Muskerry* by Padraic Colum - World Premiere.

Vincent Dowling as Edmund Tyrone and T.P. Mc Kenna as James Tyrone Jr. in the 1959 Irish Premiere of Long Day's Journey into Night *by Eugene O'Neill.*

PHOTO: NATIONAL THEATRE ARCHIVES

MAY SIXTH

MAY SEVENTH

1985, *Glengarry Glen Ross* by David Mamet - **Abbey Premiere.**

Scene from the 1985 World Premiere of A Thief of a Christmas *by Tom Murphy.*

PHOTO: FERGUS BOURKE

MAY EIGHT

2001, ***Blackwater Angel*** by Jim Nolan - World Premiere.

MAY NINTH

1983, ***The Great Hunger*** by Tom Mac Intyre - World Premiere.

MAY TENTH

1976, ***Hedda Gabler*** by Henrik Ibsen - **Abbey Premiere.**

Excerpt from the diaries of Joseph Holloway.

Courtesy of The National Library of Ireland

have accumulated for illustrating the book would alone incite interest among people interested in the subject. Mr. Aubrey Donai... could, upon hearing that I had completed my work, paid me the compliment of saying that he knew no one who was better informed about his father, no one he would rather have undertaken the work, I hope to go abroad this summer and, if I can so arrange, I may drop in unexpectedly some day upon you + Mrs Lawrence. With sincere regards, I am, yours very truly, Townsend"

Saturday. I walked down into town by St Brunswick St & read announcement at Green's Theatre that there would be no performance on account of the death of King Edward VII. Went on to the Abbey where met O'Donovan going in, — a lady was making inquiries if there would performance to-day at the front door, from Mr Martin — at the time would not pay. O'Donovan & I went into Green Room. Soon after turned in, the telephone was kept busy with inquiries performances + & I intended going over to Lafayette to have them ...ten — I suggested to ...? that he ought to be letters styles forma...

1959, *The Country Boy* by John Murphy - World Premiere.

1947, *The Dark Road* by Elizabeth Connor - World Premiere.

*Scene from the 1978
production of*
The Star Turns Red
by Sean O'Casey.

PHOTO: FERGUS BOURKE

ABBEY THEATRE

Proprietors — THE NATIONAL THEATRE SOCIETY

Directors — ERNEST BLYTHE, ROIBEARD O'FARACHAIN, SEAMUS DE BHILMOT, GABRIEL FALLON

Secretary — ERIC GORMAN

MONDAY, 29TH MARCH, 1965
AND FOLLOWING NIGHTS AT 8

A JEW CALLED SAMMY

A PLAY IN THREE ACTS
BY JOHN McCANN

LATECOMERS NOT ADMITTED UNTIL END OF FIRST ACT

STALLS 10/- & 8/- ; DRESS CIRCLE 10/- & 8/- :
UPPER CIRCLE 5/- ; GALLERY 2/6.

BOOKING AT QUEENS THEATRE
BOX OFFICE OPEN 10.30 TO 6.   'PHONE 44505

Corrigan & Wilson, Ltd., Dublin

2003, *Doldrum Bay* by Hilary Fannin - World Premiere.

1974, *Sarah* by James Ballantyne - **Abbey Premiere.**

1991, *The Patriot Game* by Tom Murphy - World Premiere.

1927, *Black Oliver* by John Guinan - World Premiere.

MAY SEVENTEENTH

1979, *Petticoat Loose* by M. J. Molloy - World Premiere.

MAY EIGHTEENTH

1978, *Stephen D* by Hugh Leonard - **Abbey Premiere.**

*Ria Mooney as Mary Cavan Tyrone
and Kathleen Barrington as
Cathleen, a maid servant
in the 1959 Abbey Premiere of
Long Day's Journey into Night
by Eugene O'Neill.*

PHOTO: NATIONAL THEATRE ARCHIVES

MAY TWENTIETH

1951, *Áis na nDéithe* by Eamon Guaillí - **Abbey Premiere.**

MAY NINETEENTH

1958, *The Scythe and the Sunset* by Denis Johnston - World Premiere.

MAY TWENTY FIRST

2002, *That Was Then* by Gerard Stembridge - World Premiere.

*Fiona Shaw as Medea in the
2000 production of* Medea
*translated by Kenneth McLeish
and Frederic Raphael,
after Euripides.*

PHOTO: NEIL LIBBERT

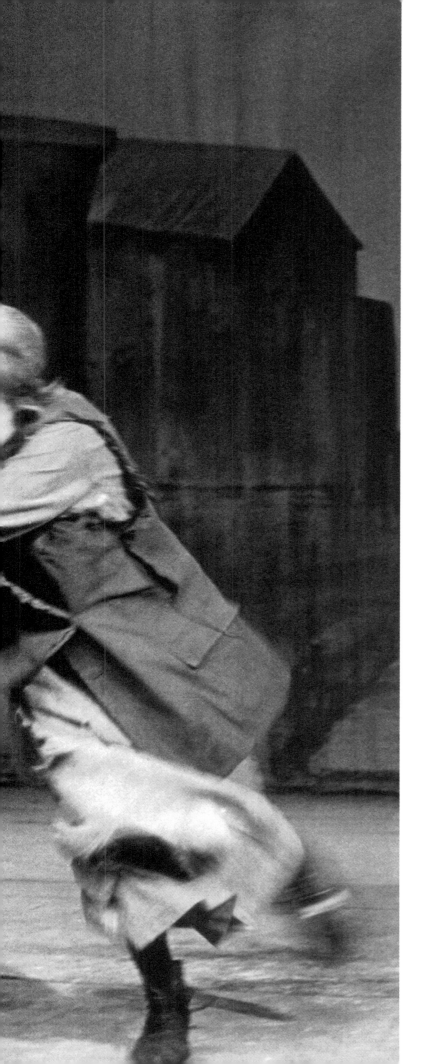

MAY TWENTY SECOND

1961, *The Honey Spike* by Bryan Mac Mahon - World Premiere.

MAY TWENTY THIRD

1972, *Bedtime Story* by Sean O'Casey - Abbey Premiere.

*Siobhan McKenna as
Bessie Burgess and
Angela Newman as
Mrs Gogan in the 1976
production of* The Plough
and the Stars *by
Sean O'Casey.*

PHOTO: FERGUS BOURKE

1920, *The Tents of the Arabs* by Lord Dunsany - World Premiere.

1993, *The Last Apache Reunion* by Bernard Farrell - World Premiere.

1980, *Endgame* by Samuel Beckett - **Abbey Premiere.**

1945, *Oighreacht Na Mara* by Walter Macken - **Abbey Premiere.**

Excerpt from the diaries of Joseph Holloway.

COURTESY OF THE NATIONAL LIBRARY OF IRELAND

MAY TWENTY EIGHT

1918, *A Little Bit of Youth* by Christian Callister - World Premiere.

MAY TWENTY NINTH

2001, *The Memory of Water* by Shelagh Stephenson - **Abbey Premiere.**

*Emmet Bergin as Cranly
and Barry McGovern
as Stephen in the 1978
production of* Stephen D
by Hugh Leonard.

PHOTO: FERGUS BOURKE

MAY THIRTIETH

1969, *The O'Neill* by Thomas Kilroy - World Premiere.

MAY THIRTY FIRST

1937, *In the Train* by Frank O'Connor and Hugh Hunt - World Premiere.

*Cyril Cusack as a waiter
and Desmond Perry as
Finch McComas in the
1978 production of*
You Never Can Tell
by G. B. Shaw.

PHOTO: FERGUS BOURKE

June

1 | 2 | 3 | 4 | 5 | 6 | 7 | 8 | 9 | 10 | 11 | 12 | 13 | 14 | 15 | 16 | 17 | 18 | 19 | 20 | 21 | 22 | 2

1994, **The Broken Jug** adapted by John Banville, after Kleist - World Premiere.

JUNE   SECOND

1 | 25 | 26 | 27 | 28 | 29 | 30

1993, **The Trojan Women** by Brendan Kennelly, after Euripides
- World Premiere.

*Helen Carey as Kate
Keller in the
2003 production of
All My Sons by
Arthur Miller.*

PHOTO: TOM LAWLOR

JUNE THIRD

JUNE FIFTH

1939, *Harlequin's Positions* by Jack B. Yeats - World Premiere.

*Ian Mc Elhinney as
Lord Illingworth and
Barry McGovern as
Sir John Pontefract in
the 1996 production of*
A Woman of no
Importance *by
Oscar Wilde.*

PHOTO: AMELIA STEIN

JUNE SIXTH

2000, *Medea* translated by Kenneth McLeish and Frederic Raphael, after Euripides - **Abbey Premiere.**

JUNE SEVENTH

1995, *Angels in America. Part One: Millennium Approaches* by Tony Kushner - **Abbey Premiere.**

Scene from the
1987 production of
Dance for your Daddy
by Tom MacIntyre.

PHOTO: FERGUS BOURKE

JUNE EIGHT

1931, *The Admirable Bashville* by G. B. Shaw - **Abbey Premiere.**

JUNE NINTH

1905, *The Land* by Padraic Colum - World Premiere.

JUNE TENTH

1998, *As The Beast Sleeps* by Gary Mitchell - World Premiere.

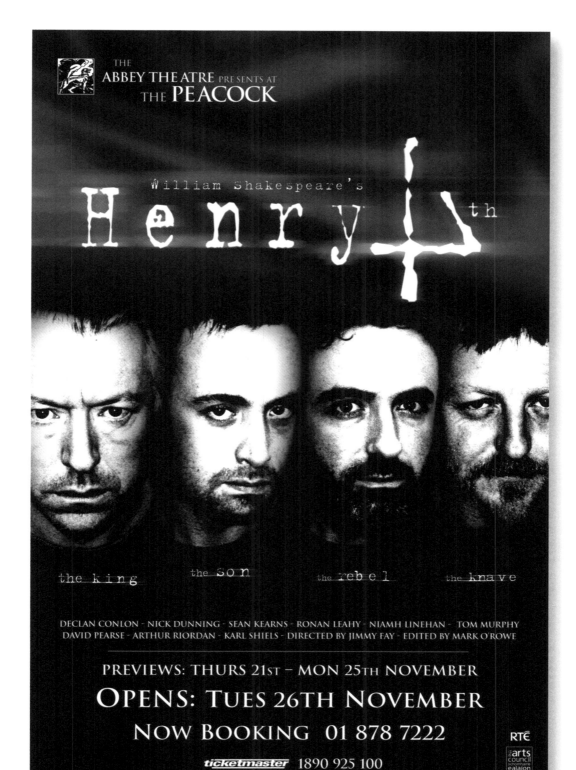

1997, *A Picture of Paradise* by Jimmy Murphy - World Premiere.

1996, *A Woman of No Importance* by Oscar Wilde - Abbey Premiere.

Colm Meaney,
Clive Geraghty and
Liam Neeson in the
1979 production of
The Death of
Humpty Dumpty
by J. Graham Reid.

PHOTO: FERGUS BOURKE

JUNE THIRTEENTH

JUNE FIFTEENTH

1988, *Ulysses* adapted by Ronnie Walsh and Anthony Cronin, after James Joyce - **Abbey Premiere.**

1969, *Night Boat from Dublin* by Harry J. Pollock - **Abbey Premiere.**

JUNE FOURTEENTH

JUNE SIXTEENTH

1976, *We do it for Love* by Patrick Galvin, performed by The Lyric Theatre, Belfast - **Abbey Premiere.**

1980, *Joycemen* by Eamon Morrissey, after James Joyce - **Abbey Premiere.**

Kathleen Barrington, Máire Ní Domhnaill and Eileen Crowe in the 1965 production of Deirdre *by W.B. Yeats.*

PHOTO: NATIONAL THEATRE ARCHIVES

JUNE SEVENTEENTH

1976, *Bless Me Father* by Eamon Kelly - World Premiere.

JUNE EIGHTEENTH

1934, *Bridgehead* by Rutherford Mayne - World Premiere.

Back: Patrick Layde, Geraldine Plunkett, Harry Brogan, Bill Foley, Eileen Crowe, Máire O' Neill, Micheál O hAonghusa. Front: Patrick Laffan and Angela Newman in the 1964 production of The Far Off Hills *by Lennox Robinson.*

PHOTO: NATIONAL THEATRE ARCHIVES

1978, *Patrick Gulliver* by Eamon Morrissey,
after Jonathan Swift - **Abbey Premiere.**

JUNE TWENTY SECOND

1988, *Snow White* by Tom Mac Intyre - World Premiere.

JUNE TWENTY THIRD

1983, *Da* by Hugh Leonard - **Abbey Premiere.**

Tom Hickey as Galileo.
in the 1981 production of
The Life of Galileo *by*
Bertolt Brecht,

PHOTO: FERGUS BOURKE

JUNE TWENTY FOURTH

1997, *A Different Rhyme* by Lorraine O'Brien - World Premiere.

JUNE TWENTY SIXTH

JUNE TWENTY FIFTH

JUNE TWENTY SEVENTH

1932, *Michaelmas Eve* by T. C. Murray - World Premiere.

*Ruth Negga as Java in
the 2003 production of*
Doldrum Bay *by
Hilary Fannin.*

PHOTO: TOM LAWLOR

JUNE TWENTY EIGHT

JUNE TWENTY NINTH

*Scene from the 2000
production of* Medea
*translated by Kenneth
McLeish and Frederic
Raphael, after Euripides.*

PHOTO: NEIL LIBBERT

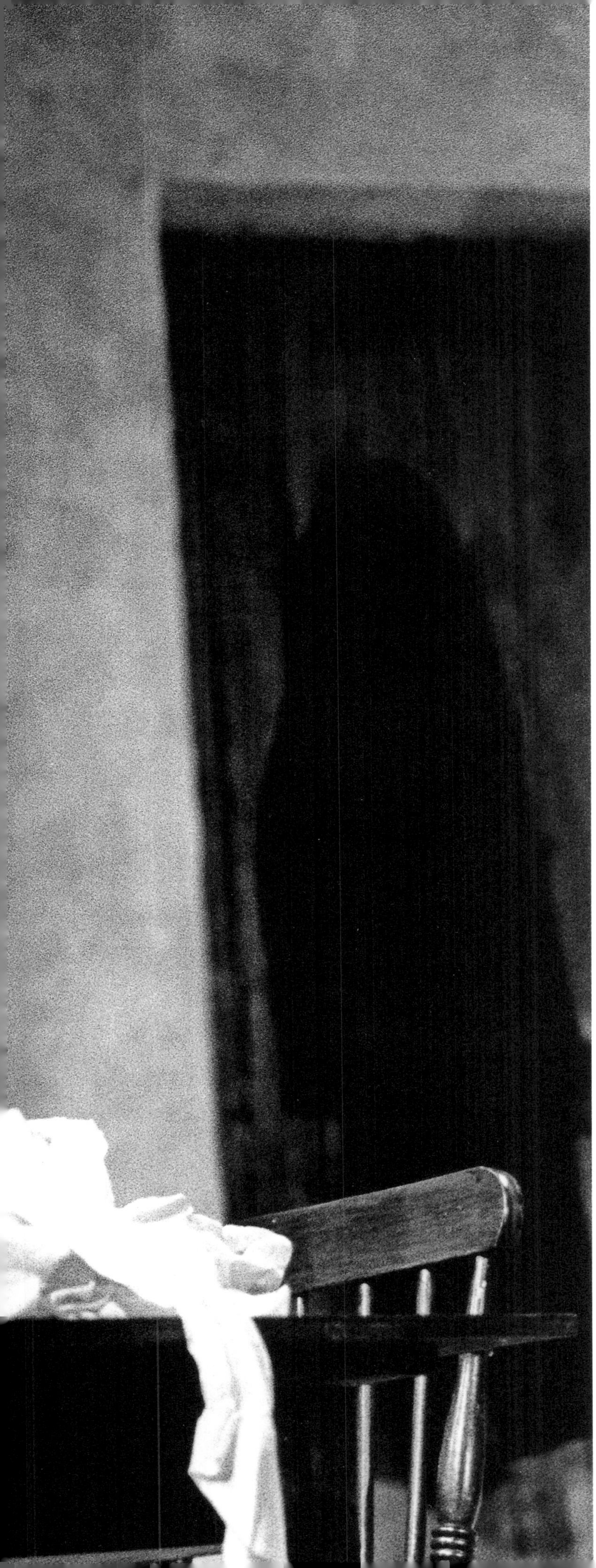

1993, *Wonderful Tennessee* by Brian Friel - World Premiere.

*Johnny Murphy as Alec
Brady and Marie Mullen
as Mother in the 1992
production of A Crucial
Week in the Life of a
Grocer's Assistant, by Tom
Murphy.*

PHOTO: JONATHAN HESSION

Patrick Layde, George Webb, Peadar Lamb, Paddy O'Callaghan, Veronica Duffy, Kathleen Barrington, Bernadette McKenna, Bosco Hogan and Philip O'Flynn in the 1972 production of The Iceman Cometh *by Eugene O'Neill.*

PHOTO: DERMOT BARRY

4 | 2 5 | 2 6 | 2 7 | 2 8 | 2 9 | 3 0 | 3 1

JULY FIRST

JULY SECOND

Des Nealon as Fr. Francis McInerney
in the 1995 production of A Little
Like Paradise *by Niall Williams.*

PHOTO: AMELIA STEIN

1979, *The Story Goes* by Eamon Kelly - World Premiere.

1912, *The Bogie Men* by Lady Gregory. The Abbey Company
at the Royal Court Theatre, London - World Premiere.

*Flo MacSweeney
as Hands in the 1990
production of* Nacht
und Traume
by Samuel Beckett.

PHOTO: FERGUS BOURKE

JULY SIXTH

1942, *The Whip Hand* by B. G. Mac Carthy - World Premiere.

JULY SEVENTH

1931, *Scrap* by J. A. O'Brennan - World Premiere.

*A scene from the 1974
production of*
The Resistable Rise
of Arturo Ui
by Bertolt Brecht.

PHOTO: FERGUS BOURKE

2003, *The Wild Duck* adapted by Frank McGuinness,
after Henrik Ibsen - World Premiere.

1934, *On The Rocks* by G. B. Shaw - **Abbey Premiere.**

The **Abbey Theatre** presents
at The **Peacock**

The
Wild Duck

By Henrik Ibsen
A New Version by Frank McGuinness
Directed by László Marton

Previews Thurs 3rd July - Mon 7th July
Opens Tues 8th July

Performance Times
Mon - Sat 7.30pm (Sat Matinee 2.00pm)

NOW BOOKING

Abbey Box Office
01 878 7222 No Booking Fee

RTÉ

ticketmaster **0818 719300** (subject to booking fee)

arts
council
schomhairle
ealaíon

1969, *Soldier* by Liam Lynch - World Premiere.

1948, *The Drums Are Out* by John Coulter - World Premiere.

*Joe Neal as Pettersen and
Eleanor Methven as
Berta Sorby in the 2003
production of*
The Wild Duck *adapted
by Frank McGuinness,
after Henrik Ibsen.*

PHOTO: TOM LAWLOR

2000, *Alice through the Looking Glass* adapted by Jocelyn Clarke, after Lewis Carroll. Peacock Partner Production - **Abbey Premiere.**

1958, *Ar Buille A hOcht* by Marjorie Watson - **Abbey Premiere.**

1993, *The Cavalcaders* by Billy Roche - World Premiere.

1956, *Early and Often* by John McCann - World Premiere.

Ingrid Craigie and Fedelma Cullen in the 1993 production of The Last Ones *by Maxim Gorky.*

PHOTO: AMELIA STEIN

JULY SEVENTEENTH

1972, *An Evening In* by Paul Shepherd - **Abbey Premiere.**

JULY EIGHTEENTH

1969, *Swift* by Eugene McCabe - World Premiere.

Nuala Hayes, May Cluskey,
Maureen Toal, Kate Flynn and
Martina Stanley in a publicity
shot for the 1982 production of
The Factory Girls *by*
Frank McGuinness.

PHOTO: FERGUS BOURKE

THE ABBEY

The National Theatre

opens 12 march

booking: 878 72 22 ticketshop: 456 95 69

juno and the paycock
by seán o'casey

returns by public demand

'a juno for the nineties' sunday independent

1987, *Lady G* by Carolyn Swift - **Abbey Premiere.**

1984, *Rockaby* by Samuel Beckett - **Abbey Premiere.**

1957, *The Less We Are Together* by John O'Donovan - World Premiere.

*Scene from the 1993
production of*
The Honey Spike
by Bryan Mac Mahon.

PHOTO: AMELIA STEIN

JULY TWENTY FOURTH

1968, *Happy as Larry* by Donagh Mac Donagh - **Abbey Premiere.**

JULY TWENTY SIXTH

1967, *An Beal Bocht* adapted by Seán Ó Briain,
after Flann O'Brien - World Premiere.

JULY TWENTY FIFTH

1955, *Blood is Thicker than Water* by John McCann - World Premiere.

JULY TWENTY SEVENTH

1994, *Asylum! Asylum!* by Donal O'Kelly - World Premiere.

*Peadar Lamb, Eamon Kelly, Joe
Dowling and Bosco Hogan
(seated) in the 1973 production
of* The Death and Resurrection
of Mr. Roche *by Thomas Kilroy.*

PHOTO: FERGUS BOURKE

JULY TWENTY EIGHT

1952, *Home Is The Hero* by Walter Macken - World Premiere.

JULY TWENTY NINTH

1946, *The Righteous Are Bold* by Frank Carney - World Premiere.

Dervla Kirwan as
Laura Wingfield in the
1990 production of
The Glass Menagerie
by Tennessee Williams.

PHOTO: TOM LAWLOR

1934, *The King of the Great Clock Tower* by W. B. Yeats - World Premiere.

1967, *Red Roses For Me* by Sean O'Casey - **Abbey Premiere.**

Ingrid Craigie as Sheila Moorneen and Stephen Brennan as Ayamonn Breydon in the 1980 production of Red Roses for Me, *by Sean O'Casey.*

PHOTO: FERGUS BOURKE

August

1 | 2 | 3 | 4 | 5 | 6 | 7 | 8 | 9 | 10 | 11 | 12 | 13 | 14 | 15 | 16 | 17 | 18 | 19 | 20 | 21 | 22 |

AUGUST FIRST

1960, *Anyone Could Rob A Bank* by Thomas Coffey - World Premiere.

AUGUST SECOND

1 | 2 5 | 2 6 | 2 7 | 2 8 | 2 9 | 3 0 | 3 1

*Damien Matthews as
George Yolland and
Fiona McGeown as
Máire in the 2000
production of*
Translations
by Brian Friel.

PHOTO: TOM LAWLOR

AUGUST FOURTH

1958, ***A Change of Mind*** by John O'Donovan - World Premiere.

AUGUST THIRD

AUGUST FIFTH

1940, ***The Rugged Path*** by George Shiels - World Premiere.

Harry Brogan as Sir Toby Bumper in the 1973 production of The School for Scandal *by Richard B. Sheridan.*

PHOTO: FERGUS BOURKE

AUGUST SIXTH

1962, *The Enemy Within* by Brian Friel - World Premiere.

AUGUST SEVENTH

1979, *Upstarts* by Neil Donnelly - World Premiere.

*May Cluskey as Mrs.
Heegan and Patrick Laffan
as Harry Heegan in the 1972
production of* The Silver
Tassie *by Sean O'Casey.*

PHOTO: DERMOT BARRY

AUGUST EIGHT

1972, *Eye-Winker, Tom-Tinker* by Tom Mac Intyre - World Premiere.

AUGUST NINTH

1974, *Struensee* by John McKendrick - World Premiere.

AUGUST TENTH

1938, *Purgatory* by W. B. Yeats - World Premiere.

Nick Dunning as Julian and Julia Lane as June in the 2002 production of That Was Then *by Gerard Stembridge.*

PHOTO: PAUL MCCARTHY

1981, *Scenes from an Album* by William Trevor - **Abbey Premiere.**

AUGUST TWELFTH

1935, *The Silver Tassie* by Sean O'Casey - **Abbey Premiere.**

Declan Conlon as Michael
Carney, Don Wycherley as
Harry Carney and Cathy Belton
as Betty in the 2001 production
of A Whistle in the Dark
by Tom Murphy.

PHOTO: PAUL MCCARTHY

AUGUST THIRTEENTH

1929, *Fighting the Waves* by W. B. Yeats - World Premiere.

AUGUST FOURTEENTH

1975, *Figuro in the Night* by Sean O'Casey - **Abbey Premiere.**

AUGUST FIFTEENTH

1932, *Things That Are Caesar's* by Paul Vincent Carroll - World Premiere.

AUGUST SIXTEENTH

1926, *Mr. Murphy's Island* by Elizabeth Harte - World Premiere.

*John Olohan as Seamus
in the 1989 production
of* The Death and
Ressurection of
Mr. Roche
by Thomas Kilroy.

PHOTO: FERGUS BOURKE

AUGUST SEVENTEENTH

1959, *Stranger, Beware* by Thomas Coffey - World Premiere.

AUGUST EIGHTEENTH

1941, *Remembered For Ever* by Bernard Mc Ginn - World Premiere.

*Malcolm Douglas, Philip
O'Sullivan, John Olohan
and Michael Grennell in the
1982 production of
The Hidden Curriculum
by J. Graham Reid.*

PHOTO: FERGUS BOURKE

A Comedy by OLIVER GOLDSMITH

She Stoops to Conquer

OR

THE MISTAKES OF A NIGHT
in an Irish setting by Thomas Murphy

Opening Thursday 11 February, 1982
(previews 9 & 10)

Stephen Brennan, Eileen Colgan, Ingrid Craigie,
Donagh Deeney, Malcolm Douglas,
Geoff Golden, Fiona MacAnna,
Niamh McAnally, Gerard McSorley,
Eamon Morrissey, Paul Moore,
Brid Ni Neachtain, Micheal O Briain,
Philip O'Flynn, Joan O'Hara,
John Olohan, Desmond Perry,
Godfrey Quigley.

Director
Joe Dowling
Settings & Costumes
Frank Conway
Lighting
Leslie Scott
Original Music by
Jolyon Jackson

Credit Card Booking
Tel 787179
Booking 744505

ABBEY THEATRE

1956, *Strange Occurance on Ireland's Eye* by Denis Johnston - World Premiere.

1919, *The Fiddler's House* by Padraic Colum - World Premiere.

1972, *Pull Down A Horseman* by Eugene Mc Cabe - **Abbey Premiere.**

1988, *Boss Grady's Boys* by Sebastian Barry - World Premiere.

AUGUST TWENTY THIRD

1995, *April Bright* by Dermot Bolger - World Premiere.

Sorcha Cusack as Nora
Clitheroe and Siobhan
McKenna as Bessie
Burgess in the 1976
production of The
Plough and the Stars
by Sean O'Casey.

PHOTO: FERGUS BOURKE

1931, *A Disciple* by Teresa Deevy - World Premiere.

1909, *The Shewing-Up of Blanco Posnet* by G. B. Shaw - World Premiere.

1962, *A Jew Called Sammy* by John McCann - World Premiere.

*Paul Murphy, Alan
Stanford and Kate Flynn
in the 1976 production
of* Hedda Gabler *by
Henrik Ibsen.*

PHOTO: FERGUS BOURKE

A U G U S T   T W E N T Y   E I G H T

1980, *Faith Healer* by Brian Friel - **Abbey Premiere.**

A U G U S T   T W E N T Y   N I N T H

1996, *Strawberries in December* by Antoine Ó Flatharta - World Premiere.

John Kavanagh, Edward Golden,
Philip O'Flynn, Robert Carlisle
and Joe Dowling in the
1972 production of
Prisoner of the Crown
by Richard F. Stockton.

PHOTO: DERMOT BARRY

1971, *Ulysses in Nighttown* adapted by Marjorie Barkentine, after James Joyce - **Abbey Premiere.**

AUGUST   THIRTY   FIRST

1976, *Our Town* by Thornton Wilder - **Abbey Premiere.**

*Olwen Fouéré and
Tom Hickey in the
1998 production of*
By the Bog of Cats
by Marina Carr.

PHOTO: AMELIA STEIN

September

1 | 2 | 3 | 4 | 5 | 6 | 7 | 8 | 9 | 10 | 11 | 12 | 13 | 14 | 15 | 16 | 17 | 18 | 19 | 20 | 21 | 22 | 2

4 | 25 | 26 | 27 | 28 | 29 | 30

SEPTEMBER FIRST

1941, *The Fire Burns Late* by P. J. Fitzgibbon - World Premiere.

SEPTEMBER SECOND

1919, *The Saint* by Desmond Fitzgerald - World Premiere.

*Frank McCusker
as Nick in the
1993 production of*
The Last Apache
Reunion
by Bernard Farrell.

PHOTO: TOM LAWLOR

1911, *The Love Charm* by William Boyle - World Premiere.

SEPTEMBER THIRD

SEPTEMBER FIFTH

1923, *Apartments* by Fand O'Grady - World Premiere.

1953, The Paddy Pedlar by M. J. Molloy - World Premiere.

Elizabeth Bracken, Sandra O'Malley and Ciarán McCauley in the 2000 co-production of Alice Through the Looking Glass *adapted by Jocelyn Clarke, after Lewis Carroll. Peacock Partner Production.*

1979, *The Death of Humpty Dumpty* by J. Graham Reid - World Premiere.

1942, *An Apple A Day* by Elizabeth Connor - World Premiere.

*David Kelly as Jack in the
1997 World Premiere of
Give me your answer, do!
by Brian Friel.*

PHOTO: AMELIA STEIN

SEPTEMBER EIGHT

1924, *Autumn Fire* by T. C. Murray - World Premiere.

SEPTEMBER NINTH

1974, *The Happy Go-Likeable Man* by Jim Sheridan, after Moliere
- World Premiere.

SEPTEMBER TENTH

1951, *The Devil A Saint Would Be* by Louis D' Alton, World Premiere.

*J. A. O'Rourke as The Saint in the 1908
production of The Well of the Saints by
J. M. Synge.*

PHOTO: NATIONAL THEATRE ARCHIVES

SEPTEMBER ELEVENTH

1913, *Sovereign Love* by T. C. Murray - World Premiere.

SEPTEMBER TWELFTH

1927, *Oedipus At Colonus* adapted by W. B. Yeats, after Sophocles
- World Premiere.

*Scene from the 2002
production of*
The Plough and the Stars
by Sean O'Casey.

PHOTO: TOM LAWLOR

SEPTEMBER THIRTEENTH

SEPTEMBER FIFTEENTH

1930, *Let The Credit Go* by Bryan Cooper - World Premiere.

SEPTEMBER FOURTEENTH

SEPTEMBER SIXTEENTH

1970, *King of the Castle* by Eugene Mc Cabe - **Abbey Premiere.**

1935, *A Deuce O' Jacks* by F. R. Higgins - World Premiere.

*Edward Golden as
Samson and Ray
McAnally as John Fibbs
in the 1981 production
of* The Passing Day *by
George Shiels.*

PHOTO: FERGUS BOURKE

1967, *King Of The Barna Men* by George Fitzmaurice - **Abbey Premiere.**

*Scene from the 1990
production of
The Silver Tassie
by Sean O'Casey.*

PHOTO: FERGUS BOURKE

The National Theatre presents

at the Abbey

The Tempest

by William Shakespeare

The Arts Council
An Chomhairle Ealaíon
RTÉ

| Previews | Dec 3rd 1999 | Opens | Dec 8th 1999 |
| Bookings | 01 878 7222 | TICKETMASTER | 01 456 9569 |

1938, *The Great Adventure* by Charles I. Foley - World Premiere.

1931, *The Cat and the Moon* by W. B. Yeats - World Premiere.

1978, *Mr Yeats and the Death of Cuchulain* by Jim Fitzgerald - **Abbey Premiere.**

SEPTEMBER TWENTY SECOND

1941, *Swans and Geese* by Elizabeth Connor - World Premiere.

SEPTEMBER TWENTY THIRD

1958, *The Risen People* by James Plunkett - World Premiere.

Inside the auditorium of the first Abbey Theatre.

PHOTO: NATIONAL THEATRE ARCHIVES

1917, *The Parnellite* by Seamus O'Kelly - World Premiere.

1988, *Carthaginians* by Frank Mc Guinness - World Premiere.

1916, *John Bull's Other Island* by G. B. Shaw - **Abbey Premiere.**

1983, *Imeachtai na Saoirse* by Antoine Ó Flatharta - **Abbey Premiere.**

*Pauline McLynn as
Androcles in the 1993
production of
The Trojan Women
by Brendan Kennelly,
after Euripides.*

PHOTO: AMELIA STEIN

SEPTEMBER   TWENTY   EIGHT

1981, *Gaeilgeoirí* by Antoine Ó Flatharta - **Abbey Premiere.**

SEPTEMBER   TWENTY   NINTH

1983, *The Gigli Concert* by Tom Murphy - World Premiere.

*Barry Mc Govern in the
1987 production of*
Sarcophagus *translated by
Michael Glenny, after
Vladimir Gubaryev.*

PHOTO: FERGUS BOURKE

1982, *Kolbe* by Desmond Forristal, **Abbey Premiere.**

Maureen Delany, Arthur Shields
and Sara Allgood in the 1925
production of The Playboy of the
Western World *by J. M. Synge.*

PHOTO: NATIONAL THEATRE ARCHIVES

*Sara Kestelman as Nell and Justine Mitchell as Grace in
the 2003 production of* The Shape of Metal
by Thomas Kilroy.

October

1 | 2 | 3 | 4 | 5 | 6 | 7 | 8 | 9 | 10 | 11 | 12 | 13 | 14 | 15 | 16 | 17 | 18 | 19 | 20 | 21 | 22 | 2

OCTOBER FIRST

2002, *Ariel* by Marina Carr - World Premiere.

OCTOBER SECOND

1980, *Canaries* by Bernard Farrell - World Premiere.

Maureen Potter as Mary Quirke in the 1992 production of Moving *by Hugh Leonard.*

PHOTO: TOM LAWLOR

1979, *A Life* by Hugh Leonard - World Premiere.

1968, *The Tailor and Ansty* adapted by P. J. O'Connor, after
Eric Cross, World Premiere.

1994, *The Mai* by Marina Carr - World Premiere.

*Maureen Toal as
Kate Keller and
John Kavanagh as
Chris Keller in the
1981 production of
All My Sons by
Arthur Miller.*

PHOTO: FERGUS BOURKE

OCTOBER SIXTH

1976, *Tea and Sex and Shakespeare* by Thomas Kilroy - World Premiere.

OCTOBER SEVENTH

1975, *The Sanctuary Lamp* by Tom Murphy - World Premiere.

Des Cave, Eamon Morrissey,
Fiona Mac Anna, Desmond
Perry and Clive Geraghty in
the 1980 production of
Canaries by Bernard Farrell.

PHOTO: FERGUS BOURKE

OCTOBER EIGHT

1981, *The Silver Dollar Boys* by Neil Donnelly - World Premiere.

OCTOBER NINTH

1980, *Nightshade* by Stewart Parker - World Premiere.

OCTOBER TENTH

1967, *Borstal Boy* by Brendan Behan and Frank MacMahon - World Premiere.

*Janet Moran as Dona Sabelita
in the 2000 production of
Barbaric Comedies adapted by
Frank McGuinness, after
Ramón María del Valle-Inclán.*

PHOTO: DOUGLAS ROBERTSON

1984, *Cúirt an Mhéan Oíche* adapted by Siobhan McKenna, after Brian Merriman - World Premiere.

1977, Travesties by Tom Stoppard - **Abbey Premiere.**

Fedelma Cullen and Kate Flynn in the 1982 production of A Doll's House *by Henrik Ibsen.*

PHOTO: FERGUS BOURKE

OCTOBER THIRTEENTH

1993, **Brothers of the Brush** by Jimmy Murphy - World Premiere.

OCTOBER FOURTEENTH

1998, **Amazing Grace** by Michael Harding - World Premiere.

OCTOBER FIFTEENTH

1997, **Melonfarmer** by Alex Johnston - World Premiere.

OCTOBER SIXTEENTH

1979, **The Nightingale and not the Lark**, by Jennifer Johnston
- World Premiere.

*Rosaleen Linehan as
Bernarda and Olwen Fouéré
as Angustias in the 2003
production of* The House of
Bernarda Alba *translated by
Sebastian Barry, after
Federico García Lorca.*

PHOTO: TOM LAWLOR

OCTOBER SEVENTEENTH

1912, *The Magnanimous Lover* by St. John Ervine - World Premiere.

OCTOBER EIGHTEENTH

1948, *The King of Friday's Men* by M. J. Molloy - World Premiere.

*Shaun Curry, Brian Dennehy,
Ernest Perry Jr., Sean McGinly,
Clive Geraghty and Donald
Moffat in the 1992 production
of* The Iceman Cometh *by
Eugene O'Neill.*

PHOTO: TOM LAWLOR

Brian Friel

Philadelphia, Here I Come !

Opening Thursday 13 May
- 29 May (previews 11 & 12)
Returns 6 - 24 July

Stephen Brennan,
May Cluskey,
Donagh Deeney,
Clive Geraghty,
Geoffrey Golden,
Nicholas Grennell,
Tom Hickey,
Marie Kean,
Peadar Lamb,
Billie Morton,
Ray McAnally,
Gerard McSorley,
Macdara Ó Fátharta,
Philip O'Flynn

Director
Joe Dowling
Design
Frank Conway
Lighting
Tony Wakefield

Sets and costumes
sponsored by
IRISH SHELL LTD

 Credit Card Booking
Tel 787179
Booking 744505

ABBEY THEATRE

1959, *Súgán Sneachta* by Máiréad Ní Ghráda - **Abbey Premiere.**

1970, *Tá Crut Nua ar na Sléibhte* by Micheál Mac Liammóir
and Liam Ó Briain - **Abbey Premiere.**

1941, *Lover's Meeting* by Louis D' Alton - World Premiere.

1928, *The Far Off Hills* by Lennox Robinson - World Premiere.

1973, *Mise Raifteirí an File* by Criostóir O Floinn - **Abbey Premiere.**

Gabriel Byrne and Nuala
Hayes in the 1978 production
of Diarmuid agus Gráinne
by Micheál Mac Liammóir.

PHOTO: FERGUS BOURKE

OCTOBER TWENTY FOURTH

OCTOBER TWENTY SIXTH

1922, *Grasshopper* by Padraic Colum - **World Premiere.**

OCTOBER TWENTY FIFTH

OCTOBER TWENTY SEVENTH

1934, *Macbeth* by William Shakespeare - **Abbey Premiere.**

1910, *Birthright* by T. C. Murray - **World Premiere.**

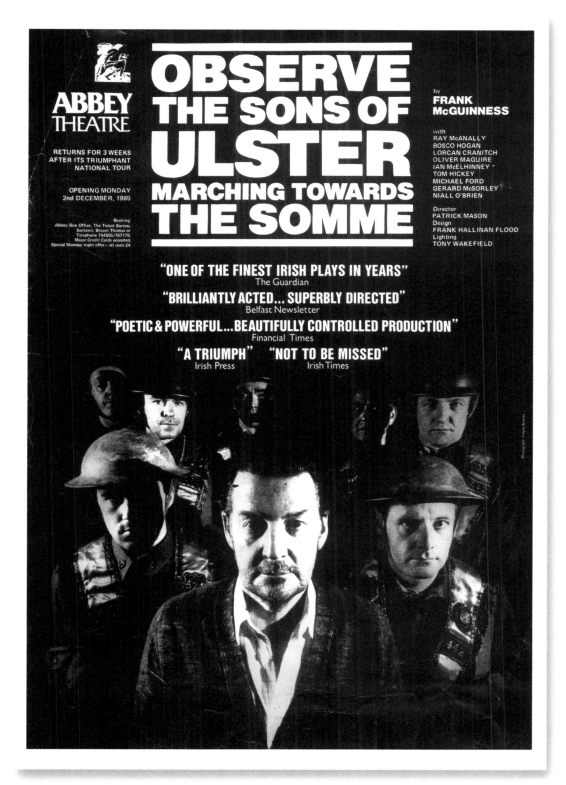

OCTOBER TWENTY EIGHT

OCTOBER TWENTY NINTH

1929, *The Gods of the Mountain* by Lord Dunsany - World Premiere.

*Kathleen Barrington, Tom
Hickey, Fiona McAnna,
Billie Morton, Garrett
Keogh and Paul Murphy in
the 1979 production of*
I Do Not Like
Thee, Dr. Fell
by Bernard Farrell.

PHOTO: FERGUS BOURKE

1972, *Philadelphia, Here I Come!* by Brian Friel - **Abbey Premiere.**

OCTOBER THIRTY FIRST

1907, *Dervorgilla* by Lady Gregory - World Premiere.

Rehearsal shot from the 1971 production of Macbeth *by William Shakespeare.*

PHOTO: DERMOT BARRY

November

1 | 2 | 3 | 4 | 5 | 6 | 7 | 8 | 9 | 10 | 11 | 12 | 13 | 14 | 15 | 16 | 17 | 18 | 19 | 20 | 21 | 22 | 2

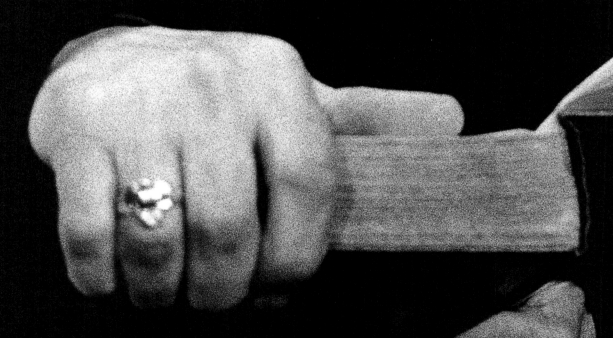

NOVEMBER FIRST

1976, *The Hard Life* adapted by Pat Layde, after Flann O'Brien
- World Premiere.

NOVEMBER SECOND

1987, *Later* by David Pownall - **Abbey Premiere.**

*John Cowley as Father
Dolan in the 1990
production of* The
Shaughraun *by Dion
Boucicault.*

PHOTO: FERGUS BOURKE

STOP
THE EXPORT
OF HORSES

1919, *Androcles and the Lion* by G. B. Shaw - **Abbey Premiere.**

NOVEMBER THIRD

NOVEMBER FIFTH

1947, *Diarmuid agus Gráinne* by Micheál Mac Liammóir
- **Abbey Premiere.**

1996, *Something's in the Way* by John McArdle - World Premiere.

*Pat Laffan as Sammy Rosenberg and
Donal McCann as Alphonsus
Cartney in the 1965 production of
A Jew Called Sammy by John
McCann.*

Photo: National Theatre Archives

N O V E M B E R   S I X T H

1967, *Play* by Samuel Beckett, **Abbey Premiere.**

N O V E M B E R   S E V E N T H

1932, *The Big Sweep* by M. M. Brennan - World Premiere.

Siobhan McKenna as Juno Boyle and Fedelma Cullen as Mary Boyle in the 1979 production of Juno and the Paycock *by Sean O'Casey.*

PHOTO: FERGUS BOURKE

1926, *The Importance of Being Earnest* by Oscar Wilde - **Abbey Premiere.**

1936, *The Wild Goose* by Teresa Deevy - World Premiere.

1988, *O Ananias, Azarias and Misael* by Jennifer Johnston - **Abbey Premiere.**

Sean Kearns as Gordon in the 1997 production of In a Little World of our Own *by Garry Mitchell.*

PHOTO: AMELIA STEIN

1909, *The Image* by Lady Gregory - World Premiere.

1962, *Hut 42* by John B. Keane - World Premiere.

Philip O'Flynn as Da, Clive Geraghty as Charlie and Ray McAnally as Drumm in the 1983 production of Da *by Hugh Leonard.*

PHOTO: FERGUS BOURKE

1933, *Grogan and the Ferret* by George Shiels - World Premiere.

1922, *Crabbed Youth and Age* by Lennox Robinson - World Premiere.

1916, *Partition* by D. C. Maher - World Premiere.

1911, *The Marriage (An Pósadh)* by Douglas Hyde - **Abbey Premiere.**

Deirdre Donnelly as Constance Constantia and Niall Buggy as Hector de la Mare in the 1992 production of Drama at Inish *by Lennox Robinson.*

PHOTO: AMELIA STEIN

NOVEMBER SEVENTEENTH

1977, *A Pagan Place* by Edna O'Brien - **Abbey Premiere.**

NOVEMBER EIGHTEENTH

1946, *The Visiting House* by M. J. Molloy - World Premiere.

*Scene from the 1983
production of
Translations
by Brian Friel.*

PHOTO: FERGUS BOURKE

The ABBEY THEATRE *Presents*

The House *of* Bernarda Alba

by Federico Garcia Lorca
in a New Translation by Sebastian Barry

PREVIEWS: Wednesday 9th to Saturday 12th April 2003

OPENS: Monday 14th April 2003

RTÉ

NOW BOOKING: 01 878 7222

 1890 925 100

the arts council schomhairle ealaíon

1951, *Innocent Bystander* by Seamus Byrne - World Premiere.

1988, *Big Maggie* by John B. Keane - **Abbey Premiere.**

1990, *Prayers of Sherkin* by Sebastian Barry - World Premiere.

LENNOX
ROBINSON

NOVEMBER TWENTY SECOND

1966, *Tarry Flynn* adapted by P. J. O'Connor, after Patrick Kavanagh
- World Premiere.

NOVEMBER TWENTY THIRD

1964, *A Page Of History* by Eilís Dillon - World Premiere.

Joan O'Hara as Grandma
Fraochlain and
Derbhle Crotty as Millie
in the 1994 production
of The Mai
by Marina Carr.

PHOTO: AMELIA STEIN

1906, *Deirdre* by W. B. Yeats - World Premiere.

1928, *King Lear* by William Shakespeare - **Abbey Premiere.**

1940, *Peeping Tom* by Frank Carney - World Premiere.

1923, *The Glorious Uncertainty* by Brinsley Mac Namara - World Premiere.

THE
ABBEY THEATRE PRESENTS

ALL MY SONS

BY ARTHUR MILLER

DIRECTED BY: JOE DOWLING

PREVIEWS: MONDAY 10TH – THURSDAY 13TH FEBRUARY
OPENS: FRIDAY 14TH FEBRUARY

RTÉ   **NOW BOOKING: 01 878 7222**   ticketmaster 1890 925 100   the arts council schomhairle ealaíon

NOVEMBER TWENTY EIGHT

1996, **Black Ice** by Thomas Mc Laughlin - World Premiere.

NOVEMBER TWENTY NINTH

2000, **The Hunt for Red Willie** by Ken Bourke - World Premiere.

Andrew Bennett as Lucien,
Catherine Mack as Death
and Chris McHallem as
Henry in the 1999
production of The Map
Maker's Sorrow *by*
Christopher Lee.

PHOTO: AMELIA STEIN

1915, *John Ferguson* by St. John Ervine - World Premiere.

*Eamon Morrissey as Kelly
in the 1989 production of*
The Death and
Resurrection of Mr.
Roche *by Thomas Kilroy.*

PHOTO: FERGUS BOURKE

December

D E C E M B E R   F I R S T

1969, *Waiting for Godot* by Samuel Beckett - **Abbey Premiere.**

D E C E M B E R   S E C O N D

1970, *The Plebians Rehearse the Uprising* by Gunther Grass - **Abbey Premiere.**

Owen Roe as The
Irish Man in the 2001
production of
The Gigli Concert
by Thomas Murphy.

PHOTO: AMELIA STEIN

2001, *On Such As We* by Billy Roche - World Premiere.

1934, *Six Characters in Search of an Author* by Luigi Pirandello - **Abbey Premiere.**

1972, *Saint Joan* by G. B. Shaw - **Abbey Premiere.**

Garrett Keogh as Fuso Negro in the 2000 production of Barbaric Comedies *in a new version by Frank McGuinness, after Ramón María del Valle-Inclán.*

PHOTO: DOUGLAS ROBERTSON

1931, *The Dreaming of the Bones* by W. B. Yeats - World Premiere.

1911, *Red Turf* by Rutherford Mayne - World Premiere.

Peter O'Toole as Vladimir,
Eamon Kelly as Pozzo and
Donal McCann as
Estragon in the 1969
production of Waiting for
Godot *by Samuel Beckett.*

PHOTO: DERMOT BARRY

1906, *The Shadowy Waters* by W. B. Yeats - **Abbey Premiere.**

1976, *End of Term* by Maeve Binchy - World Premiere.

G.B.Shaw

To J.H. from F.L.

*Dawn Bradfield as Katie
and Marie Mullen as
Maggie in the 2001
production of
Big Maggie by
John B. Keane.*

PHOTO: PAUL MCCARTHY

1917, *Blight* by "A & O" (Oliver St. John Gogarty) - World Premiere.

1988, *The Gentle Island* by Brian Friel - Abbey Premiere.

Scene from the 1977 production of The Old Lady Says No! *by Denis Johnston.*

PHOTO: FERGUS BOURKE

DECEMBER THIRTEENTH

1916, *The Whiteheaded Boy* by Lennox Robinson - World Premiere.

DECEMBER FIFTEENTH

1988, *Tall Tales* by Jim O'Keeffe, Collette Farrell and Sean Campion
- World Premiere.

DECEMBER FOURTEENTH

1911, *The Countess Cathleen* by W. B. Yeats - **Abbey Premiere.**

DECEMBER SIXTEENTH

1982, *Petty Sessions* by Bernard Farrell - World Premiere.

*Ronnie Drew and
Luke Kelly in the 1972
production of* Richard's
Cork Leg *by
Brendan Behan.*

PHOTO: DERMOT BARRY

DECEMBER SEVENTEENTH

1918, *Atonement* by Dorothy Macardle - World Premiere.

DECEMBER EIGHTEENTH

1980, *The Man who came to Dinner* by George S. Kaufmann and Moss Hart
- Abbey Premiere.

Ruth O'Bríain, Marie Mullen,
Phelim Drew, Brendan Gleeson,
Eamon Kelly and Ruth McCabe in
the 1991 production of
The Plough and the Stars
by Sean O'Casey.

PHOTO: FERGUS BOURKE

DECEMBER NINETEENTH

1972, *The Golden Apple* adapted by Tomás Mac Anna, after Lady Gregory
- **Abbey Premiere.**

DECEMBER TWENTIETH

2000, *Tartuffe* adapted by Declan Hughes, after Moliere - World Premiere.

*Lorcan Cranitch as Prospero
and Dawn Bradfield as
Miranda in the
1999 production of
The Tempest by
William Shakespeare.*

PHOTO: AMELIA STEIN

DECEMBER TWENTY FIRST

1977, *Wild Oats* by John O'Keeffe - **Abbey Premiere.**

1924, *Old Mag* by Kenneth Sarr - World Premiere.

DECEMBER TWENTY THIRD

1968, *An Baile Seo 'Gainne* adapted by Michael Judge, after An Seabhac
- World Premiere.

Pauline Flanagan as
Mommo in the 2001
production of
Bailegangaire
by Tom Murphy.

PHOTO: PAUL McCARTHY

DECEMBER TWENTY FORTH

DECEMBER TWENTY SIXTH

1953, *Bláithín agus an Mac Rí*, Gaelic Pantomime - World Premiere.

DECEMBER TWENTY FIFTH

DECEMBER TWENTY SEVENTH

1904, *On Baile's Strand* by W. B. Yeats and *Spreading the News* by Lady Gregory - World Premieres.

Excerpt from the diaries of Joseph Holloway.

... gentile, Mr Dave Clarke) Duke of Wurtemberg (Mr Robert Faulkner)
Prince of Nassau (Mr F C Overton) General Talmash (Mr Don Ireland)
General Sir John Lanier (Mr C Durant) Colonel Kirke (Mr Abel Williams)
Colonel Parker (Mr R Talmont) Colonel Villars (Mr Fennan)
Rapin (Mr ? Weldon) Lord Justice Porter (Mr ?)
ingsby (Mr Charles Wells) Lord Sydney, Mr Thomas L Rooney) Hans Anstein
dam (Mr Harry Richardson) Terry Toper (Mr James O'Brien) Parrah ...
(Mr D ? Daly) Duisy Rafferty (Mr O H Fielden) Lady Honor de Burgho
(Mrs Brome (Hylton) Lady Rose (Mrs Maude Tremayne) Molly (Mrs
Arnold) & Silly (Blake ... Mrs Frances Kelly).   Dec 26.

-2) Tuesday — Opening of the Abbey Theatre, Abbey Street, by the ...
... by W B Yeats (first time on any stage) with ... written by ... one act play
... Fay) Concobar (Mr George Roberts) Daire (Mr W Donald) Fintain (Mr Frank
... Seumas O'Sullivan) Sarah (Mr T ? Fay) & Young ... (Mr F Walker) Young
... old king, Mr ... Allgood, Esposito, Ormesley, Mr Fawey Walker ...
... less Keegan, Stuart, Power, & Wright). Spreading the News, comedy ...
... one act) Lady Gregory, first time on any stage ... Mrs Fallon (Mrs
... ford) Mrs Tully (Miss Esposito) Mrs Tarpley (Mrs Fawey) Bartley ...

559

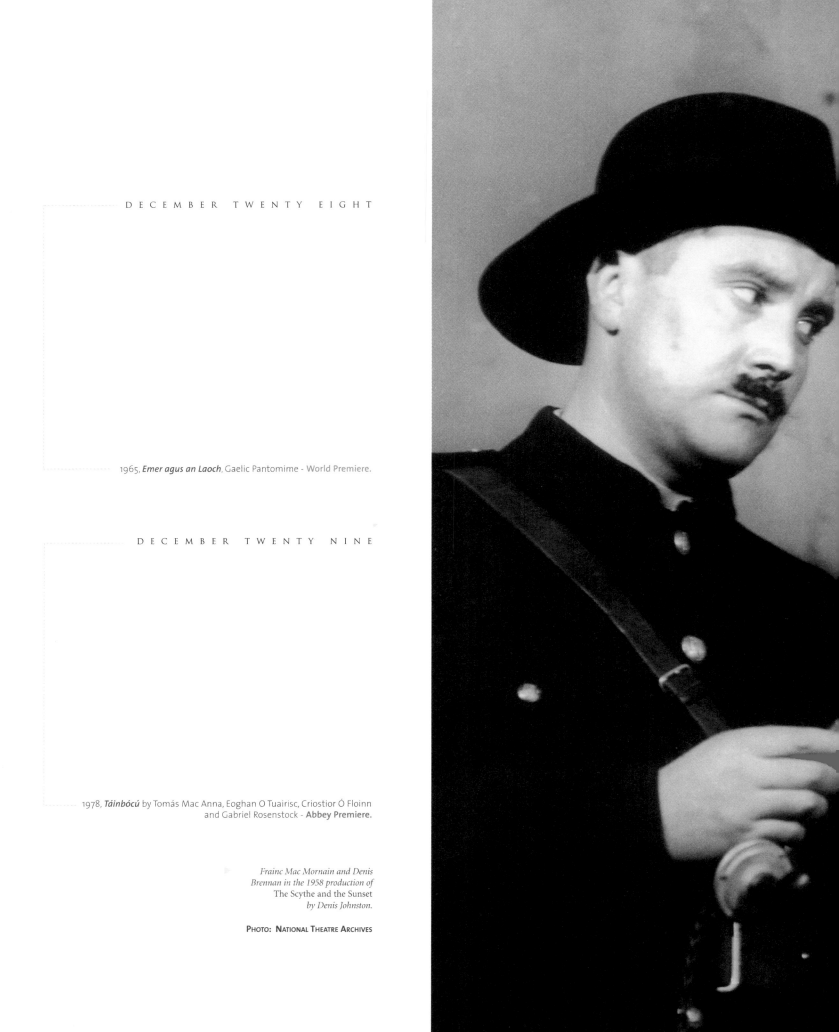

DECEMBER TWENTY EIGHT

1965, *Emer agus an Laoch*, Gaelic Pantomime - World Premiere.

DECEMBER TWENTY NINE

1978, *Táinbócú* by Tomás Mac Anna, Eoghan O Tuairisc, Criostior Ó Floinn and Gabriel Rosenstock - **Abbey Premiere.**

Frainc Mac Mornain and Denis Brennan in the 1958 production of The Scythe and the Sunset *by Denis Johnston.*

PHOTO: NATIONAL THEATRE ARCHIVES

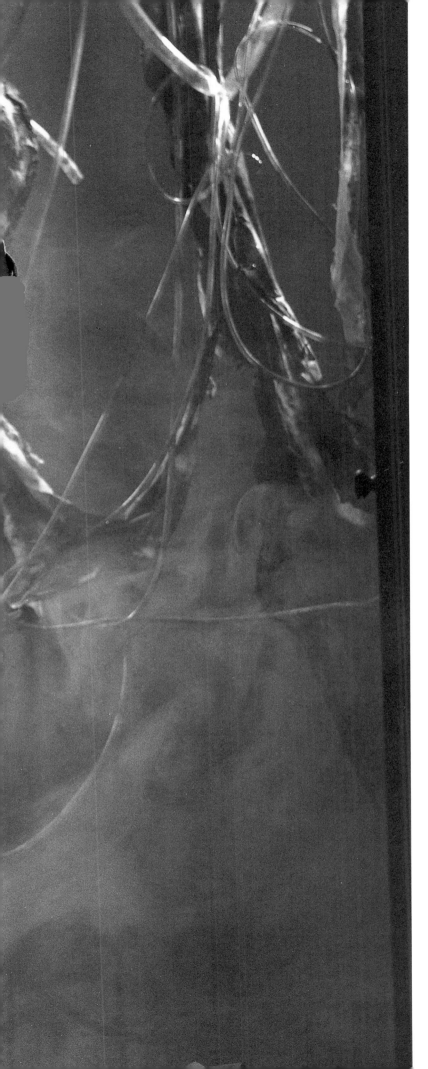

DECEMBER THIRTIETH

1985, *A Thief of a Christmas* by Tom Murphy - World Premiere.

DECEMBER THIRTY FIRST

1923, *The Old Woman Remembers* by Lady Gregory - World Premiere.

Ned Dennehy as Fergus Mac Phellimey a Pooka, in the 1998 production of At Swim-Two-Birds *adapted by Alex Johnston, after Flann O'Brien.*

PHOTO: AMELIA STEIN

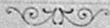

Programme for the 1905 production of A Christmas Hamper by Mr and Mrs McHardy-Flint at the Abbey Theatre. E. deValeria (sic) playing Dr. Kelly.

THE HOLLOWAY DIARIES

Selected Extracts

Joseph Holloway was the architect engaged by Annie Horniman to remodel the Abbey Theatre. Holloway was an enthusiastic theatre goer for over fifty years. His diaries, some two hundred manuscript volumes, together with his collection of programmes, posters and other theatrical memorabilia, form one man's unique record of the Dublin Theatre scene in the first half of the twentieth century. The extracts below are Holloway's contemporaneous reactions to four significant events in the early history of the Abbey, the first opening night, the 'Playboy' riots of 1907, the Players strike of 1916 and the 'Plough' riots of 1926.

Tuesday, December 27th. 1904

At the beginning of the pretty little Abbey Theatre, the Messrs. Fay covered themselves with glory, both as the guiding spirits of the new theatre and as actors. The night was a memorable one, and the house was thronged and genuinely enthusiastic. The spirit of enthusiasm was in the air from the first, and everyone went away wishing for more . . . All three plays were completely successful, and the audience dispersed delighted; and the opening night of the Abbey Theatre must be written down a great big success. Long life to it, and to the Society which gave it birth through the generous impulse of Miss Horniman!

Tuesday, January 29th 1907

. . . Arrived at the Abbey . . . A number of youths were dimly seen in the stalls . . . I noticed that the youths in the stalls were mostly under the influence of drink (and learned that the management had allowed them in for nothing to back up the play that the crowded pit had come there to howl down). This precious gang of noisy boys hailed from Trinity, and soon after The Playboy commenced one of their number . . . made himself objectionable and was forcibly removed by Synge and others, after a free fight amongst the instruments of the orchestra. W. B. Yeats came before the curtain . . . and made a speech "inviting a free discussion on the play on Monday night next in the theatre." Shortly after the commencement of the police-protected play, a remark from the pit set the college boys to their feet and for a moment they looked like going for those in the pit, but didn't. The uproar was deafening . . . One of the theatre's bullies removed by the people who wanted him in struck me as a funny sight. This set the noise in motion, and W. B. Yeats

came on the scene and with raised hand secured silence. He refered to the removal of one drunken man and hoped all that were sober would listen to the play. The noise continued, and shortly after a body of police led on by W. B. marched out of the side door from the scene dock and ranged along the walls of the pit. Hugh Lane now made himself very conspicuous by pointing out some men in the pit and demanding their arrest as disturbers of the peace. Yeats also was busy just now as a spy aiding the police in picking out persons disapproving of the glorification of murder on the stage.

A gent addressed the audience from the stalls, and the students with Hugh Lane in their midst behaved themselves like the drunken cads they were. At the end chaos seemed to have entered the Abbey, and the college youths clambered onto the seats and began the English national anthem, while those in the body of the hall sang something else of home growth. I felt very sad while the scene continued. The college boys had ultimately to be forcibly ejected by the police, and they marched off in a body singing, police-protected, to the college.

Monday, May 29th. 1916

About eight o' clock I strolled down to the Abbey to find the doors had just been closed and some small knots of people were standing about in eager conversation, and a boy in front of the stalls entrance handed out handbills to the people as they arrived at the theatre. The slip read, "To the patrons of the Abbey Theatre. The Players regret having to disappoint their Public this week, as they will NOT APPEAR at the Theatre under the present Manager, MR. ST. JOHN ERVINE. Full

particulars will appear in the Press" . . . When asked was this the last of the Abbey, I said, "Not at all. The Abbey has come to stay. No Ervine can slay it, had it not had nine or more lives, it would have been slain long ago by the vagaries of Yeats and Gregory, but the public refused to let it die."

Thursday, February 11th 1926

The protest of Tuesday night having no effect on the management, a great protest was made to-night, and ended in almost the second act being played in dumb show, and

pantomiming afterwards. People spoke from all parts of the house, and W. B. Yeats moved out from the stalls during the noise, and Kathleen O'Brennan, who came in afterwards, told me Yeats went round to *The Irish Times* office to try to have the report of the row doctored. On his return to the theatre, he tried to get a hearing on the stage, but not a word he spoke could be heard . . . I am sorry to say that I was incorrect in my judgement as to what Abbey audiences could stand when I told George O'Brien . . . that they would stand even the devils in Hell exhibiting their worst pranks in silence sooner than make another objectionable play like *The Playboy* burst into notoriety by their disapproval. But, alas, to-night's protest has made a second *Playboy* of *The Plough and the Stars*, and Yeats was in his element at last . . .
Few really like the play as it stands, and most who saw it are in sympathy with those who protested. Some of the players behaved with uncommon roughness to some ladies who got on the stage, and threw two of them into the stalls. One young man thrown from the stage got his side hurt by the

piano. The chairs of the orchestra were thrown on the stage, and the music on the piano fluttered and some four or five tried to pull down half of the drop curtain . . .

The Holloway Diaries are the property of the Trustees of the National Library of Ireland and have been reproduced with their permission. All marginalia are reproduced courtesy of the National Library of Ireland.

YOUR NOTES

YOUR NOTES

Published in 2003 by

The Abbey Theatre,

26 Lower Abbey Street,

Dublin 1, Ireland.

ISBN 0-9545269-3-7

Design Paul Rattigan

Produced by Zeus Creative, Dublin.